# IMPROVING
# READING SKILLS
## ACROSS THE CONTENT AREAS

# IMPROVING READING SKILLS

## ACROSS THE CONTENT AREAS

*Ready-to-Use
Activities and
Assessments for
Grades 6-12*

# REBECCA ROZMIAREK

**CORWIN PRESS**
A SAGE Publications Company
Thousand Oaks, California

*For information:*

Corwin Press
A Sage Publications Company
2455 Teller Road
Thousand Oaks, California 91320
www.corwinpress.com

Sage Publications Ltd
1 Oliver's Yard
55 City Road
London EC1Y 1SP
United Kingdom

Sage Publications India Pvt. Ltd.
B-42, Panchsheel Enclave
Post Box 4109
New Delhi 110 017  India

Printed in the United States of America on acid-free paper

*Library of Congress Cataloging-in-Publication Data*

Rozmiarek, Rebecca.
Improving reading skills across the content areas : ready-to-use activities and assessments for grades 6-12 / Rebecca Rozmiarek.
        p. cm.
Includes bibliographical references and index.
ISBN 1-4129-0459-5 (cloth) — ISBN 1-4129-0460-9 (pbk.)
    1. Content area reading. 2. Reading (Secondary) 3. Education, Secondary—Activity programs.  I. Title.
LB1050.455.R69 2006
428.4'071'2—dc22

                                2005022087

This book is printed on acid-free paper.

05   06   07   08   10   9   8   7   6   5   4   3   2   1

| | |
|---|---|
| *Acquisitions editor:* | Rachel Livsey |
| *Editorial assistant:* | Phyllis Cappello |
| *Production editor:* | Sanford Robinson |
| *Copy editor:* | Dan Hays |
| *Typesetter:* | C&M Digitals (P) Ltd. |
| *Indexer:* | Karen A. McKenzie |
| *Cover designer:* | Rose Storey |
| *Graphic designer:* | Lisa Miller |

# Contents

# Preface

Reading provides an opportunity to journey to another world and make sense of things that happen in other times and places. Reading is also an opportunity to connect new information to what is already known. Many middle and high school students today, however, struggle to take advantage of the opportunities that reading provides. These students do not see that reading is the essential component to being successful academically. This book provides teachers across the curriculum with the strategies and activities necessary for helping students be successful readers who are able to acquire knowledge in each of their academic classes. The activities presented in this book are appropriate for all levels grades 6–12, including gifted and talented, special education, and English as a second language.

The activities that teachers encounter in this book are based on the work of such leading reading researchers as Michael Pressley and anchored in the standards published by the International Reading Association and the National Council of Teachers of English. Although this book is grounded in theory and research, the emphasis is on practical techniques and activities for meeting the needs of students in the area of reading across the curriculum. These classroom-proven techniques can be immediately incorporated into the content-area teacher's curriculum. This book provides teachers with a multitude of ways for reaching all students and improving their reading proficiency in all subject areas. Teachers will learn how to use double-entry journals, text coding, bookmarking, and questioning strategies to help students be more engaged readers. In addition, teachers are provided with various activities to foster independence, self-reflection, and motivation in students. Teachers across the curriculum will gain a wealth of ideas for helping students respond to text, evaluate and discuss what they read, and assess their own growth.

Each chapter presents the teacher with a skill overview, a detailed description of relevant subskills, several practical skill-building activities, and an assessment rubric. The skill-building activities illustrate specifically for the teacher how to use the instructional approaches across the content areas. The vignettes give examples of real students using the activities to make sense of text, respond to text, and increase their overall comprehension of text. The resource section of this book provides blank reproducibles so that teachers can incorporate the activities immediately into their own classroom. Teachers from every content area will be able to immediately see how to use the activities presented to help their students be successful readers.

# ACKNOWLEDGMENTS

First, I acknowledge the students and faculty at Bel Air Middle School who have offered me feedback throughout the years on how to make strategic reading activities more helpful in raising student achievement. I owe an immense debt of gratitude to my principal, Nancy Reynolds, for allowing me to take risks and design ongoing professional development, particularly in the area of reading for my school. I also thank my colleagues and friends, Christina O'Neill and Pat Ritz, with whom I serve on the Literacy Team at my school. Christina and Pat work tirelessly to meet the needs of the students and teachers in our school, and their dedication is inspirational.

In addition, I thank my good friend Kim Henry for encouraging me to share my ideas with a wider audience through consulting and publishing.

I thank my husband, Daniel Rozmiarek, for the countless hours he has spent supporting my efforts to create lessons and assessments for teachers. I acknowledge my children, Sarah, Anna, and Joshua, for inspiring me to be a good teacher in hopes that our schools will provide a bright future for all our children.

I thank my mom for teaching me how to read and how to think deeply about text information. She was my first teacher, and her dedication to education is the reason I became a teacher.

Finally, I thank teachers everywhere for their continuing service to the field of education in these challenging times. I commend the efforts that teachers make toward strengthening their current programs and designing reading instruction that will help our middle and high school readers be able to comprehend, analyze, and evaluate what they read and be able to apply those skills across the curriculum. Our students desperately need the strategies and skills necessary to be proficient readers in the 21st century.

The contributions of the following reviewers are gratefully acknowledged:

Jeanne Guthrie
Teacher (retired)
Overland Park, KS

Arlene Myslinski
ELL Teacher
Buffalo Grove High School
Buffalo Grove, IL

Diane M. Holben
Director of Research, Planning, and Accountability
Allentown School District
Allentown, PA

Anne Roede Giddings
Assistant Superintendent
Ansonia Public Schools
Ansonia, CT

# About the Author

**Rebecca Rozmiarek** is an author, national presenter, and classroom teacher who has worked with both students and teachers across the curriculum in grades 6–12. As a literacy specialist, she works with teachers at Bel Air Middle School in Harford County Public Schools, Maryland, to develop and implement effective reading strategies across the curriculum. In addition, she teaches struggling learners how to use strategies to acquire text information. She is a teacher consultant for the Maryland Writing Project at Towson University and a presenter for the Bureau of Education and Research. She is a member of both the Instructional Leadership Team and the School Improvement Team at her school. She works to make data-based decisions about instruction, particularly in the area of reading. In collaboration with colleagues at her school, she designs and implements ongoing staff development for teachers across the curriculum. Her ideas are research based but practical and ready to use immediately in the classroom.

**CORWIN
PRESS**

The Corwin Press logo—a raven striding across an open book—represents the union of courage and learning. Corwin Press is committed to improving education for all learners by publishing books and other professional development resources for those serving the field of PreK–12 education. By providing practical, hands-on materials, Corwin Press continues to carry out the promise of its motto: **"Helping Educators Do Their Work Better."**

# 1

## Introduction to Reading in Grades 6–12

### WHAT IS READING?

Current reading research incorporates the basic tenets of cognitive psychology and schema theory (Gillet & Temple, 1990). In the current model, readers are active participants who use before, during, and after reading strategies to engage with the text. By using the reading process, readers are more than passive participants who merely receive information from the text. As readers interact with the text, they construct meaning by using their prior knowledge (Marr & Gormley, 1982; Pearson, 1985) to make predictions and thus comprehend the text.

The focus on readers as active rather than passive participants in the reading process has resulted in a much more comprehensive understanding of the term *reading*. In addition, our current climate of accountability has also added layers of meaning to the concept of what it means to be a proficient reader. According to No Child Left Behind legislation (2002), the term reading is a complex system of gaining meaning from print that requires students to

- Acquire and maintain the motivation to read
- Understand unfamiliar words
- Read fluently
- Access background information and vocabulary to allow for reading comprehension
- Use appropriate strategies to understand text

## WHAT IS THE READING PROCESS?

Middle and high school teachers across the curriculum must teach students how to acquire each of the necessary reading skills through the reading process (Spiro, 1968). There are specific kinds of questions that the proficient reader will ask at each stage of the process. The following is an example of the kinds of thinking that proficient middle and high school students will do as they engage in the reading process:

### The Reading Process

#### Before Reading Activities and Questions

Begin by looking at the title, illustrations, captions, graphs, and charts.
Overview the text structure and length.
Ask yourself: "What do I already know?"
Review prior knowledge and make predictions: "What do I expect to learn?"
Determine purpose: "What will I have to do with this information?"

#### During Reading Activities and Questions

Determine key points in order to summarize as you read.
Enjoy what you are reading!
Predict what you will learn next.
Ask yourself: "Do I understand what I am reading?"
Revisit your purpose for reading and ask: "What am I learning?"
Target new information and link it to what you already know.

#### After Reading Activities and Questions

Ask yourself: "What is the main idea of the selection?"
Now use your knowledge and evidence from the text to complete the task.
Consider other interpretations of text.
Help your understanding by using a dictionary if necessary.
Offer to discuss your understanding of the text with another classmate.
Reflect on how you will use the text information in your life.

## WHAT DEFINES AN EXPERT READER?

When students consistently use a set of transactional strategies (Pressley, Brown, Van Meter, & Schuder, 1995) in a variety of situations across the curriculum throughout the school year, their reading proficiency will increase. In essence, *transactional* simply means the application of strategies with different kinds of text of varying difficulty levels in all instructional settings. At the outset of transactional learning, students are prompted to use comprehension and work attack strategies. Children learn to use these strategies across a variety of text types in several instructional settings, including reading groups that focus on high-quality literature. As a student reads, the teacher prompts him or her to use comprehension and word attack strategies. As time goes on, however, students are expected to internalize the strategies and apply them independently in all content-area and literature-based classrooms.

The strategies that expert readers must acquire include

- Setting a purpose for reading
- Connecting to prior knowledge
- Determining the meaning of words not understood or recognized
- Identifying significant information in the text
- Visualizing text information
- Asking questions to develop a deeper understanding
- Drawing conclusions and making inferences
- Analyzing text structure
- Evaluating the author's viewpoint

The idea that students must acquire strategies that they are able to use independently is one that is also shared by the International Reading Association (IRA) and the National Council of Teachers of English (NCTE). To participate in our democracy as informed citizens, IRA and NCTE have stipulated through their standards (1996) that students must be able to read a wide range of texts; apply a wide range of strategies to comprehend, interpret, evaluate, and appreciate texts; and become highly reflective and critical members of a literate society.

## WHO ARE TEACHERS OF READING?

Teachers of reading are all teachers who interact with students to assist them in acquiring and integrating new knowledge. The kinds of teachers who are teachers of reading include but are not limited to literature, science, history, civics, economics, math, home economics, technology education, computer science, art, music, and physical education teachers. All subject areas require students to internalize a certain skill level and knowledge base. Therefore, teachers of all subject areas are teachers of reading.

## WHAT IS THE ESSENTIAL VOCABULARY WITH WHICH TO TALK ABOUT TEXT?

As students engage actively with text by using the reading process, it is essential that they develop a common language with which to talk about text. In a highly literate secondary classroom, teachers must formulate comprehension questions, discussions, creative activities, and various forms of assessment that utilize the vocabulary that expert readers use. As students discuss text and interact with text in various ways, they will gain a greater facility with the following terminology:

| | |
|---|---|
| Analyze | Draw a conclusion or make a judgment based on the text information |
| Audience | The target group for a message |
| Author | The creator of text |
| Cite | Quote or refer to an author's work to support or prove an idea |
| Describe | Use words to create a mental picture of a person, place, object, or idea |
| Elaborate | Clarify using multiple details and examples |
| Evaluate | Judge based on evidence, and use support to give the good and bad points |
| Explain | Identify reasons or causes |
| Inference | A conclusion drawn from logical reasoning |
| Interpret | Explain the meaning of text in your own words |
| Justify | Use examples to support a concept or belief |
| Paraphrase | Put in your own words |
| Passage | A portion of text (paragraph(s) or verse(s)) |
| Position | An author's attitude, opinion, or viewpoint in an argument |
| Predict | Make an educated guess about what will happen next |
| Quotation | Exact words from the text punctuated with quotation marks |
| Relevant | Connected in an obvious way to the topic |
| Response | A detailed reaction to text (personal, analytical, etc.) |
| Significant | Important information |
| Summarize | Condense the main points using as few words as possible |
| Support | Provide details or examples to back up your opinion |
| Text features | Ways authors enhance text (graphics, photos, sidebars, and headings) |
| Text structure | Writing patterns authors use to convey meaning |
| Text | All author-created materials, in both print and nonprint media |

There are many components to building a solid foundation for reading. Students must acquire reading strategies that they use with automaticity as they engage in the reading process. To facilitate the acquisition of reading strategies, middle and high school teachers must create a learning environment in which students are exposed to a wide variety of texts and therefore motivated to become highly literate members of our democratic society. When such learning environments are created, students learn and achieve at the highest levels of performance.

# 2

# Setting a Purpose
# for Reading

## SKILL OVERVIEW

Whenever readers select text, they have an explicit purpose. It may be that they want to find out what movies are playing over the weekend and they check the local paper. It may be that they have an assignment to complete for a particular class and need to read a story or book to fulfill the demands of the assignment. Middle and high school students must be able to identify their own purposes for reading as well as reading for an assigned purpose. Teachers must expose students to the idea that people read for different purposes that include reading to

- Be entertained, informed, or persuaded
- Learn a new skill or process
- Evaluate the author's viewpoint
- Solve problems
- Form an opinion
- Generate questions for further research about the topic or concept
- Gather information for a discussion
- Reflect on and extend personal experience and prior knowledge

When students are engaging in the reading process, it is important that they remember their purpose for reading so that they can sort and organize the new information, connect it to their initial purpose for reading, reexamine their purpose for reading, and be able to articulate and justify how the information they have gained helps them achieve their purpose for reading.

# SUBSKILLS

## Selecting Text

Once students know and understand their purpose for reading, they should be given opportunities to select texts that will help them to achieve their purpose. Students need to be taught how to preview the text; skim for main ideas and supporting details; make note of headings and subheadings; critically analyze graphic features; and read carefully the back cover, inside cover, and any other surface information that will help them to determine the appropriateness of the text.

## Choosing Effective Strategies

Being able to set the purpose for reading is a vital first step toward developing strategic reading skills. Students need to be able to skim and scan effectively to quickly locate information. They need to be able to read carefully to gain full comprehension and read critically to analyze or interpret the author's intent. These are just some of the skills that students need to acquire to meet the purpose for reading. Make sure to expose students to text coding, double-entry journals, and anticipation guides in order for them to read for entertainment, read to find information, or reflect on the author's purpose.

## Solving Problems

One of the most compelling purposes for reading is reading to solve a problem. Have students generate topics of interest and problems that concern them. These problems can be related to local, state, national, or international issues. Have students read from many nonfiction sources to solve the problem or at least gain information to better understand the issue.

## Forming an Opinion

Another purpose for reading that is highly motivating for students is reading to form an opinion. Middle and high school students have their own ideas about many topics. As teachers, we need to coach the students in researching different viewpoints to form an intelligent opinion, one that they can back up with statistics, details, and more specific information.

## Skimming for Facts

When students have identified a motivating and focused purpose for reading, model for them how to skim for facts. Students must be able to read and gain information from a multitude of sources. To tackle as many sources as possible, students will need to be able to skim information quickly, discern which information matches their purpose for reading, and decide which information they are going to go back to and study carefully to gather more information.

## Learning New Ways to Express Ideas in Writing

As students are reading, make sure to emphasize to them that they are also writers. Students must understand that when they read and think about how the author is affecting them, they will better understand how to affect the readers of their writing. Teach them to be critical readers who are able to identify organizational patterns in text, text features, key vocabulary, and rhetorical techniques.

## Revising Purposes for Reading

After students have established their initial purpose for reading, have them generate a question. As they read and attempt to answer the question, have the students revise their purpose for reading by refining and revising their initial question. Inform the students that expert readers follow this same process. By establishing and adjusting purposes for reading, students will better learn how to be strategic thinkers and problem solvers while reading.

## Using Self-Generated Criteria to Select Reading Material

As teachers, we often present students with characteristics for selecting their nonfiction reading material. As an alternative, to build independence in middle and high school students, allow the students to generate their own characteristics or criteria for choosing nonfiction material. Some examples of criteria include that the nonfiction material connects to a specific topic, contains text features, has multiple viewpoints, and is highly engaging in physical appearance and presentation. Have the students discuss these characteristics and evaluate whether or not the nonfiction material that they selected has these characteristics.

# SKILL-BUILDING ACTIVITIES

## Activity 1: Question/Answer

Begin by having the students identify their purpose for reading. Then, lead the students in generating a list of prereading questions that will help them to achieve their purpose. For example, if students are reading about the history of football and their purpose is to understand the history and know why it is important to the sport today, they may generate several questions, such as the following: (a) Who invented the game of football? (b) Where was it invented? (c) What were the initial reactions to the game? (d) How do people react to the game today? (e) What are some traditions that surround the sport? Remind the students that to answer some of the questions, they may need to make some inferences. When the students have finished, have them reflect on how the process of questioning helped them to achieve their purpose for reading.

## Activity 2: Yes/No Evaluation

This activity further structures the question/answer activity. Have students identify some topics of interest to them. Next, have them generate questions about those topics. Take them to the school library, and allow them to select text of their choice. Have students answer their initial questions. At the end of the activity, have students write a brief explanation that evaluates why they did or did not achieve their purpose. Have students compare their evaluations with a partner. This activity will also be effective if the students have been assigned a topic and directed to do research. Students will learn the importance of setting a purpose for reading and working toward achieving that purpose.

Imagine David, a seventh grader, is doing some research about ancient Rome. He has a particular interest in battles and weaponry from this time period. What follows is his evaluation.

### Yes/No Evaluation

**Purpose for Reading:** To learn about battles and weaponry from ancient Rome (1st century C.E.)

| Questions about the topic | Answers (based on reading and research) |
|---|---|
| What kinds of weapons did the ancient Romans have? | Catapult bolts, light javelins, and heavy spears |
| Why were battles fought during this time period? | 1. For glory <br> 2. To stop outsiders from invading the provinces |
| How did the Romans protect themselves? | Fabric shirts with bronze scales for armor; wooden shields with metal covers; timber or stone forts |
| Who did the Romans fight? | Barbarians |

*Yes/No Evaluation*

## Activity 3: Question/Answer/Opinion

Follow the same procedures as the question/answer strategy. This time, however, have the students write brief opinions about the topics they researched. Some helpful sentence starters include

I wonder . . .

I was confused when . . .

I enjoyed . . .

I am curious about . . .

I was surprised to learn that . . .

This information confirms what I knew about . . .

This information contradicts what I knew about . . .

I agree/disagree because . . .

Let's look at the scenario regarding David and his research on weapons used during ancient Roman battles. Whereas David asked several questions in the previous activity, this time David focuses on one question regarding weapons used in ancient Rome.

### Question, Answer, Opinion

| **Question:** . . . |
| --- |
| *What kinds of weapons did the ancient Romans have?* |
| **Answer:** |
| *Catapult bolts, light javelins, and heavy spears* |
| **Opinion:** |
| *I particularly liked learning about the weapons. It must have been very challenging to win a battle back then because the weapons seem so primitive. I was surprised that soldiers wore so much protection. It must have been hard to throw catapult bolts at the same time that you were holding a shield to protect yourself!* |

## Activity 4: Sticky Notes and Purpose for Reading Double-Entry Journal

Pass out sticky notes to the students. As they are reading, have them mark text with a P! for strong connection to purpose and a P for some connection to purpose. When students finish reading the nonfiction text, have them record the text information that corresponds with the code that they chose in the left column of a double-entry journal chart and then write a reaction to the selected text in the right column. Have the students reflect on how the information connects to their purpose for reading and their prior knowledge of the subject.

For example, Mr. Davis's ninth-grade special education science students are investigating the question, "What life is found in soil?" Before conducting a lab in which students will examine the contents of soil, Mr. Davis instructs the students to read a chapter in their science textbooks. Students use sticky notes to mark the text as described previously. Andrea, one of Mr. Davis's students, uses the sticky notes to complete her double-entry journal as follows:

### *Purpose for Reading Double-Entry Journal*

**Purpose for reading question:** What life is found in soil?

**Key:**

P! = Strong connection to purpose for reading

P = Some connection to purpose for reading

| Text information with code | How does this information connect with your purpose for reading or your prior knowledge of the subject? What questions do you have? |
|---|---|
| *Microscopic organisms live in the soil, such as bacteria, protozoa, and fungi. (P!)* | *This information directly connects to my purpose for reading. I know that all organisms serve some kind of purpose so I wonder what these small organisms do.* |
| *The soil also contains larger forms of life, such as worms, mites, spiders, slugs, and insects. (P!)* | *This information also directly answers the purpose for reading question. I wonder what the relationship is between the microscopic organisms and the bigger forms of life.* |
| *Bacteria and fungi feed on the remains of dead plants and animals in the top layer of soil, causing decay and formation of rich topsoil. (P)* | *As the reader, I already knew that bacteria and fungi live in the soil. This information extends what I already knew by stating the function of bacteria and fungi. I found this information useful because now I know the purpose of some of the microscopic organisms.* |

## Activity 5: Multiple Text Marathon

A great way to motivate students to examine multiple texts is to present them with a purpose for reading, and then take them to the school library and have them select books or articles to achieve their purpose. For example, Ms. Lothar is a sixth-grade science teacher and wants her students to learn about conserving energy and some of the best ways to conserve energy. Have them preview at least three different texts and think about how the text would help them to achieve their purpose for reading. Instruct the students to select the best text and read more deeply to acquire the necessary information.

### *Multiple Text Marathon*

| **Purpose for reading:** *To find information on the best ways for us to conserve energy.* | Best text? Place a ✓ |
| --- | --- |
| **Evaluation of Text 1:** *The Problems with Nuclear Energy* <br><br> This article will/<u>will not</u> achieve my purpose because . . . *it's mostly about radiation and how radioactive wastes are produced. It doesn't give practical ways to conserve energy.* | |
| **Evaluation of Text 2:** *Four Ways to Conserve Energy* <br><br> This article <u>will</u>/will not achieve my purpose because . . . *it describes four ways to conserve energy: geothermal energy, tidal energy, solar energy, and nuclear energy. It gives the pros and cons of each, provides comparative diagrams and charts, and gives practical tips for how to use each of these forms of energy most effectively.* | ✓ |
| **Evaluation of Text 3:** *Using Solar Panels to Build Your House* <br><br> This article will/<u>will not</u> achieve my purpose because . . . *it is not comprehensive enough in the information it provides. It does a great job describing how to build a house with solar panels and what the benefits are, but this is only one way to conserve energy. If we are going to make major gains in conserving energy, we will need a multitude of ways to protect our earth's resources.* | |

## Activity 6: Author and Me Analysis

It is important for students to understand that they read for a variety of purposes, but that authors also write for a variety of purposes. Have the students use a double-entry journal format to identify their purpose and the author's purpose. Chances are that if the student is reading to be informed, the author was also writing for the students to be informed. As students are reading, have them record important information in the left column and make connections to their purpose for reading and the author's purpose for writing in the right column. Guide the students in making inferences about the author's purpose.

Mr. Feltham's 10th-grade international studies class is learning about cultural expectations for women and girls throughout the world. The author of a particular article believes that girls everywhere in the world should have equal opportunities to learn. What follows is Cameron's worksheet analyzing this particular author:

### Author and Me Analysis

**My purpose for reading:** To look carefully at the author's viewpoint.

| Information from the text | Author's purpose |
|---|---|
| *Some girls run away from home in order to avoid getting married. Many seek refuge in churches in order to get an education.*<br><br>*Poor families make money by requiring their daughters to work as maids. Many little girls have to work when they are only four years old.* | *The author believes that it is atrocious that some girls around the world have to fight to go to school. She gives examples about various girls from around the world in order to convince the reader to share her viewpoint.* |

### Activity 7: Purpose and Problem Solving

One of the most important things for educators to do is to teach students that they can read to solve problems related to important issues. It is vital for students to know that text contains information that is highly interesting and motivating. Expose students to interesting, engaging text as often as possible. Have students use a double-entry journal format to identify as many questions as possible related to a real-word problem. Then have them read texts that help them answer the questions that they have generated. Have them record their answers in the right column of the double-entry journal. On the back of their journal, have them draw conclusions about what actions they can take to solve the real-word problem they have investigated. To create an educational atmosphere that sends the message that reading is fun, make sure to have lots of non-fiction materials available to students.

### Activity 8: Fact-Finding Mission

In content-area classrooms, one of the most common purposes for reading is to be informed. Create an atmosphere in which learning is valuable and informational text is viewed as intriguing. Using a double-entry journal format, have the students record facts and details in the left column and write a reaction in the right column. Make sure students think about why the author wanted them to learn the information, why the information will be valuable to them, and any additional questions they may have.

In the following scenario, Mr. Bennett's 10th-grade history students are learning about communication during the time of the Roman Empire. The following activity aids students in gathering ideas and facts as well as determining a reaction or response. Gillian is a student in Mr. Bennett's class, and her double-entry journal reveals her learning:

### *Fact-Finding Mission*

**Purpose for reading:** What were the forms of communication during the time of the Roman Empire?

| Ideas and facts | My reaction |
|---|---|
| *Twenty-two letters in the Latin alphabet were used (I and J, U and V were not distinguished; W and Y did not exist).* | *It's hard for me to imagine communicating without certain letters or that certain letters were interchangeable.* |
| *Books had to be copied by hand which made them extremely valuable.* | *I think we take for granted our modern-day printing. I can't imagine copying everything!* |
| *In math, Roman numerals made arithmetic very difficult especially when computing very large numbers. Arabic numbers made math much easier.* | *I never really thought about trying to solve an equation using Roman numerals. It's interesting how different cultures pick and choose from other cultures over time in order to make communication more efficient.* |

## Activity 9: Persuasion Puzzles

We are surrounded by text that is intended to be persuasive. Have students read a variety of texts that are persuasive, and show them how to analyze the author's use of rhetorical language, examples, and appeals to the audience to make his or her argument convincing. Have the students divide their paper into quadrants. In one box, have the students record text information that is persuasive. In another box, have the students identify the choices that the author made to make his or her ideas convincing. In the third box, have the students write a reaction in which they think about the choices that the author made and why those choices made the text convincing. In the last box, have the students generate questions for further study. Through discussion, allow the students to identify ideas with which they disagree or text that is not convincing.

Imagine Ms. Jenkins's seventh-grade language arts class is examining the issue about whether or not students admire athletes too much. She is concerned that such admiration could lead to students making poor decisions much like the ones that certain athletes make simply because students believe that athletes are role models. To look at this issue more closely, Ms. Jenkins had students read various articles. Leroy's worksheet from the activity is included here:

### Persuasion Puzzles

**Topic:** *Whether or not students admire athletes too much*

| Persuasive text information | Author's persuasive techniques |
|---|---|
| *Kids want to wear the clothes and eat the food that athletes eat. Because kids want to copy athletes, they might try drugs if they know that an athlete has tried drugs.* | *The author reminds the reader that athletes are on TV all the time and just because someone is on TV it doesn't make him/her special. The author asks kids to look at their parents and teachers as role models instead of athletes.* |
| **Reaction to the author's techniques** | **Questions for further study** |
| *I think the author is a little too hard on athletes. He mentions all the bad things that athletes do, like drugs, alcohol, and tattoos. He doesn't talk about all the good things athletes do. I think his harsh view could turn kids away from his opinion.* | *How many athletes actually use illegal drugs? How many athletes abuse alcohol?*<br><br>*How does the percentage of athletes who do unhealthy things compare to the percentage of athletes who don't?*<br><br>*How many athletes use their money to make charitable contributions or improve their communities?* |

### Activity 10: KWL: An Oldie but Goodie

Extending and enriching students' prior knowledge about a subject can be very beneficial in deepening their understanding. As an introductory activity to reading information on a topic that is already familiar to the students, have them sit in a circle and in round-robin fashion share something they know about the topic or concept. Record the students' prior knowledge on a KWL chart (Ogle, 1986). As an example, Mr. Ellis's 11th-grade physics class is getting ready to begin a unit on chemical bonding. He asks his students what they already know about atoms. What follows is the KWL chart they created:

*KWL Purpose Chart*

| Before reading:<br>What do you already<br>know about the topic? | Before reading:<br>What do you want<br>to know about the topic? | After reading:<br>What did you learn? |
|---|---|---|
| *An atom contains a nucleus which is its positively charged center.*<br><br>*Outside the nucleus are negatively charged electrons.*<br><br>*Atoms make up all the substances in the universe.* | *How are different substances formed?*<br><br><br><br>*How many different combinations are there?* | *Atoms of elements combine with one another to produce new and different substances called compounds.*<br><br>*The 109 elements are each made of specific types of atoms. However, there are hundreds of thousands of different substances in our world. The combining of elements creates specific substances. Atoms combine according to very specific rules and these rules are determined by the structure of each atom.* |

## Activity 11: Reading and Following Directions

Inform students that they will encounter sets of instructions, recipes, and rule books their entire lives and need to know how to read critically to create a product or learn the necessary information to know how to do something. Have students identify something that they would like to learn how to do or to make. Take them to the school library, and allow them to find resources that fit their learning objectives. Using a double-entry journal format, have the students record the step-by-step instructions in the left column in paraphrased form. Have them write a reaction by analyzing whether or not the instructions were clear. As an extension, have the students determine the effectiveness of the graphic features and identify any further questions they have based on areas of confusion in the text.

In the following scenario, Mr. Ellis's 11th-grade physics class is going to conduct a laboratory experiment in which they create a model of energy levels. He has asked the students to evaluate the clarity of the lab using the following format. What follows is Adam's analysis of directions:

### *Analysis of Directions*

**Purpose for directions:** *To create a model of energy levels.*

| Set of directions | Analysis of directions (questions, areas of confusion, things I needed to know) |
|---|---|
| *1) To represent an atom, cut a thin piece of corkboard into a circle 50 cm in diameter.* | *1. I needed to know measurement in metric and diameter. Pretty easy.* |
| *2) Insert a large colored push pin into the center to represent the nucleus.* | *2. Very clear.* |
| *3) Draw three concentric circles around the nucleus to represent the energy levels. The inner circle should be 20 cm in diameter; the second circle 30 cm; and the third 40 cm.* | *3. Again, I needed to know metric measurement and diameter. I think pictures would have helped me visualize better. I also wonder how this flat model helps me to fully conceptualize an atom.* |

### Activity 12: Text Coding

As students are reading, instruct them to use the following codes to mark important text as it relates to their purpose for reading:

AV = Author's viewpoint

AM = Author's message

* = Important information

These codes in particular will work well with persuasive text. Preview with the students examples of biased and nonbiased language, and have them look for examples in the text. In addition, review with the students the difference between fact and opinion statements, and have the students look for examples in the text.

## ASSESSING STUDENT MASTERY OF SETTING A PURPOSE FOR READING

As teachers, we understand the importance of assessing whether or not students have acquired the skill that has been taught. You may choose to use one, many, or all of the activities presented in this chapter to help students become more proficient with setting a purpose for reading. As a professional, you will make observations regarding students' acquisition of this skill, but it is also important to formally assess their knowledge and understanding. Here, you will find a generic rubric for assessing the skill of setting a purpose for reading.

## Setting a Purpose for Reading Rubric

Use this rubric to determine students' progress toward mastery of the following skill: The student sets a purpose for reading.

### Level 4—Mastery

- The student quickly and accurately states the purpose for reading.
- The student chooses appropriate materials to read to meet the purpose for reading.
- The student skims and scans effectively to quickly locate information.
- The student independently uses reading strategies to set a purpose for reading and to read for that purpose.

### Level 3—Nearing Mastery

- The student states the purpose for reading.
- The student chooses some materials to read to meet the purpose for reading.
- The student skims and scans to locate most of the important text information.
- The student uses some reading strategies to set a purpose for reading and to read for that purpose.

### Level 2—Developing

- The student states the purpose for reading when directed by a teacher.
- The student may be able to choose some materials to read to meet the purpose for reading.
- With guidance from a teacher, the student skims and scans to locate information.

### Level 1—Basic

- The student may or may not be able to state the purpose for reading.
- The student struggles to choose materials to read to meet the purpose for reading.
- The student has difficulty skimming and scanning to locate information when reading.

### Level 0—Below Basic

- The student makes no attempt to set a purpose for reading.

# 3

## Connecting to Prior Knowledge

### SKILL OVERVIEW

Middle and high school students must be proficient at accessing their prior knowledge about the subject they are learning. Review with the students what they already know about the topic and where they learned the information. Brainstorming aspects of students' life experiences related to the topic is also highly motivating. After introducing the topic, here are some questions that may help you connect with students' personal experiences:

- What memories do you have that connect with this topic?
- Have you ever seen a TV show about the topic?
- What feelings do you have in connection with the topic?
- Have you ever known someone who has told you about the topic? What was the person like?
- What concerns or interests you about the topic?

### SUBSKILLS

#### Asking Questions

Questioning is a highly effective way to access prior knowledge. The theoretical base for prior knowledge is built on the idea that we have a cognitive schema (Pearson, 1985) that contains all our prior knowledge. Questioning helps readers to connect new knowledge with their existing knowledge about a particular topic. Some sample questions include

When you think of _____, what comes to mind?

When have you heard something similar before?

What do you already know about _____?

When you hear the word(s) _____, what do you think of?

What events or ideas do you know that connect to the topic?

## Making Connections

As educators, it is vital that we understand the importance of prior knowledge in helping students master the skill of making connections. Prior knowledge is everything that a student has learned before the new learning or reading event. Students have prior knowledge about the topic, social experiences related to the topic, text structure, and reading strategies. Some students may have very limited prior knowledge in one or all areas, other students may have some knowledge, and still others may have quite a bit of knowledge. In the classroom, it is important to recognize the range of knowledge and experiences that your students have and to provide them with a wide range of strategies that allow them to connect with the various aspects of prior knowledge and to make connections between existing knowledge and new knowledge.

## Evaluating Nonfiction Materials Using Prior Knowledge

When teachers focus on a cross-curricular approach to reading, students' reading skills are immeasurably strengthened. Throughout their academic careers, students will need to locate and read a variety of nonfiction materials to access information necessary to complete their assignments in many subject areas. The following is a list of questions that students can use to help them evaluate nonfiction materials using prior knowledge:

- Is this text organized in such a way that the information makes sense?
- What can I assume about the author's purpose based on the headings and subheadings?
- How will the text features help me to understand the topic?
- How does this text compare to another text on a similar topic?
- What reading strategies will I need to use to make sense of the information?

## Reformulating and Modifying Existing Knowledge

One of the primary purposes of learning new information is to build on and clarify the existing information you have retained from earlier experiences and learning situations. Students must have many strategies available to them to help them reformulate and modify their existing knowledge. Questions students can ask themselves include

- How does this new information confirm what I know about the topic?
- How does this new information add to what I know about the topic?
- How does this new information contradict what I know about the topic?
- How does this new information change what I know about the topic?
- How does this new information change what I believe about the topic?
- What new questions do I have?

### Applying New Learning to Real-Life Situations

Prior knowledge and personal experiences help us to make sense of text information, but new text information should also help us to understand our real lives. Students need to understand that acquisition of new knowledge becomes the groundwork for future prior knowledge about a topic. Emphasize to the students that they will need to apply what they learn in school to real-life situations.

### Formulating Ideas

After students engage in a variety of activities to tap into their prior knowledge, they need to be able to connect the text to their prior knowledge both during reading and after reading. Remind the students to generate pictures in their minds, summarize, predict, and question as they read:

- What pictures come to mind when you read this information?
- What are the key points that you are learning about?
- What do you predict will happen next?
- What do you predict that you will learn about next?
- What further questions do you have?

### Constructing an Opinion

To generate their own opinion, students must develop the skill of using their prior knowledge about a topic. By teaching students to think about what they personally believe about the topic, you give the students a "built-in" purpose for reading whenever they encounter new text. Encourage students to challenge their beliefs about the topic, the author's beliefs, their teacher's beliefs, and their fellow classmates' beliefs.

#### *Generating a Personal Response*

When students can generate a personal response to text, they will become more proficient at integrating new information. Reassure students that it is natural for them to ask such questions as they read:

- How does this information relate to me?
- How does this information change what I already know?
- How might I share this information with someone else?
- How can I demonstrate my new knowledge?
- How do I feel about this information?
- How can I use this information in my life?

# SKILL-BUILDING ACTIVITIES

## Activity 1: Text Walking and Picture Talking

Text walking (Harvey & Goudvis, 2000) is a simple activity in which you lead the students through a preview of the text, but you use the metaphor of "walking and talking." Demonstrate for the students how to preview the text by starting at the beginning of the text and talking about each text feature as you encounter it and how it helps you to understand the major topics of the text. Talking aloud helps illustrate sophisticated thinking for the students.

## Activity 2: Double-Entry Journal for Prior Knowledge

Have the students begin by identifying their prior knowledge about the subject. On the left side of the journal, have the students record text information in a list format. On the right side of the journal, have the students reflect on how the information connects to their prior knowledge.

To apply the skills in this activity, Mr. Ellis, an eighth-grade science teacher, introduced his unit on early paleontology by allowing his students to examine some fossil shark teeth. After piquing the students' interest, he asked them what they knew about fossils and asked them to complete the following double-entry journal by reading from their textbook and various other sources. What follows is Adrian's double-entry journal:

### *Double-Entry Journal for Prior Knowledge*

**Topic:** *Early paleontology*

**Prior knowledge of the topic:** Fossils are the buried remains of plants and animals.

| Text information | Reader's response |
|---|---|
| What are the three most important things you have learned from the text? | What further questions do you have? |
| *Fossils are used today to figure out the relative ages of rocks, which helps us to find oil and other valuable resources.* | *What are the richest sources of oil in the world? How many fossils surround these sources?* |
| *Serious study of fossils began only about 300 years ago.* | *What prompted serious fossil study to begin?* |
| *Georges Cuvier discovered the interrelatedness of different parts of an animal's body allowing entire fossils to be restored.* | *What was the first fossil to be fully restored? Where is it located and can the general public view this fossil?* |

## Activity 3: Structured Previews

Some students benefit from an informal preview of text, but others need a more structured approach. Lead the students through a structure preview of the text by pointing out explicitly the following aspects of text: text structure, text features such as headings and subheadings, and key concepts/facts that are bolded or italicized within the text. Have the students discuss how each of these aspects of text connects to their prior knowledge and/or personal experience. A structured approach will help struggling readers access their prior knowledge of both reading and their personal life experiences connected to the text.

In the following example, Ms. Smith is instructing her students about the tenets of energy conversion. They will be reading from their textbook and a variety of other sources. To guide the students in their reading, she leads them on a structured preview of one of the texts. Excerpts from Amanda's worksheet are included here:

### *Structured Preview*

Topic: *Energy conversion*

| Text information | Questions, thoughts, reactions |
|---|---|
| **Text structure:** *This text seems to follow mostly a cause/effect structure. The text describes a car rolling down a ramp which results in its kinetic energy increasing while its potential energy decreases.* | *While the text is primarily cause/effect, it incorporates lots of description and examples to illustrate its points. The examples help me to visualize the processes and forms of energy in my mind.* |
| **Text features:** *Picture of a roller coaster to illustrate the kinetic/potential energy conversion; text box on the career of a solar engineer; picture of a basketball player illustrating the steps between maximum potential energy and maximum kinetic energy; computational chart to measure the mass and velocity of various objects and the resulting kinetic energy.* | *I really appreciated the text box about the career of solar engineers. I often wonder about what I could do with an education in science. I might like to be responsible for harnessing solar energy as an alternative to using fossil fuels. Then, again, I might want to be an artist!* |
| **Bolded vocabulary or information:** *Energy conversions* *Solar engineers* *Heat engines* | *Since the primary focus of this segment of text was on energy conversion, the choices that the author made for highlighting key vocabulary really make sense.* |

### Activity 4: Round-Robin Reflections

Begin by having the students tap into their prior knowledge. Continue by having the students record what they learned after they read. Instruct the students to reflect on their learning by identifying personal connections, evaluating the author, and generating questions that they have. Organize the students into groups of four, and have them share their reflections. As an extension, have the students look for commonalities among their reflections and report on these commonalities to the rest of the class.

### Activity 5: Predicting and Confirming

Begin by having the students preview the text and make predictions about the content. Have them create a three-column worksheet on their own lined paper. Model for the students how to create prediction statements and record them in the left column of their worksheet. Then, have the students read the text with the intention of finding information that either confirmed or contradicted their predictions. In the center column, students should write "yes" or "no" to indicate confirmation or contradiction. They may elaborate their response in the center column if they have additional comments to make. In the right column, students should explain how the information either did or did not validate their initial predictions. They can also include what surprised, confused, or disappointed them about the text information.

Let's journey to Mrs. Creighton's eighth-grade algebra class. Students are being introduced to the equation, $x + a = b$. To complete the following predicting and confirming activity, she requires the students to preview the text to generate their prediction statement. The following is an example from Aidan's worksheet:

### *Predicting and Confirming*

**Topic:** *The mathematical equation, $x + a = b$*

| Before reading<br>Prediction statement | During reading<br>Yes/no | After reading<br>Reaction statement |
|---|---|---|
| *In previewing the text, I predict that the Addition Property of Equality will be important for understanding and applying this equation.* | *Yes, I was correct. To solve an equation of the form $x + a = b$, I need to add $-a$ to both sides and simplify.* | I was surprised when . . .<br>I was confused when . . .<br>I was disappointed when . . .<br><br>*I was confused by many of the examples. In some complicated addition equations, I can use the commutative and associative properties and I am not sure I will know when to use these.* |

## Activity 6: Visual Reading Map

A visual reading map provides struggling readers with a framework for connecting the text to their prior knowledge. Have the students examine the text carefully for bolded words, headings, subheadings, graphs, charts, diagrams, illustrations, photographs, and captions. Then, have the students draw a picture that represents their prior knowledge of the subject and information they gained from the preview. After reading, have the students explain to a partner how the text information either did or did not confirm their prior knowledge of the subject.

## Activity 7: Creating a Reading Action Plan

Langer (1995) created this strategy to assess the students' depth of understanding of the topic. Have the students identify as many words as they can that associate with the topic about which they will be reading. Then, have the students identify how they know the words. Through discussion, the students clarify and refine their connections and understandings. You can also ask the students to use the words they have generated to summarize their prior knowledge and identify what they hope to learn from the reading.

To illustrate this activity, let's examine Mr. Conway's seventh-grade life science focus on preserving the plants at a pond's surface. Mr. Conway has received a revitalization grant for his school and as a result has the opportunity to build a pond for his school. He plans to involve his students in this project and is going to require them to do some preliminary reading before they began the project. The following is Jeremy's reading action plan as generated in Mr. Conway's class:

### A Reading Action Plan

**Topic:** *Preserving plants at a pond's surface*

| Words you know that are connected to the topic | What do you think you know about these words? |
| --- | --- |
| *Algae* | *Algae is a kind of plant that floats on the top of a pond.* |
| *Ferns and fronds* | *Fronds are the leaves on a fern.* |
| *Roots* | *Roots typically anchor a plant in soil. I don't know what roots are like in water plants.* |
| *Pond surface* | *Ponds are typically peaceful unless there is a storm. There aren't waves or other currents to contend with in order to protect plant life.* |

**Write a summary of what you think you know about the topic:**

*I know that many ponds have plant life including ferns and algae. I don't know if ferns and algae are healthy for a pond. I know that it's important for a pond to have healthy plant life in order to support other life organisms in the pond.*

**What do you expect to learn?**

*I expect to learn about how plant life survives on the surface of a pond. I want to learn this information so that I can help Mr. Conway create a healthy pond for our school.*

**What did you learn?**

*I learned that some pond plants have trailing roots but some have no roots at all. The water's surface can be beaten by winds which can result in waves that destroy pond plants. I learned that algae can develop and spread so quickly that it can cover a pond's surface and block valuable sunlight to the plants beneath it. I did not learn ways to protect pond plants, but knowing Mr. Conway, that information is next!*

## Activity 8: Viewpoint Synthesizer

Middle and high school students must have the ability to synthesize various viewpoints and generate their own opinion based on the information they have gathered. To build this skill, incorporate the viewpoint synthesizer into everyday instruction. Begin by having the students use their prior knowledge to generate an opinion of the topic about which they will be reading. Then, have students fold their notebook paper into quadrants. During and after reading, have the students identify a different viewpoint related to the text information in each of the four boxes. These viewpoints could include those of the author, their teacher, another source, and another classmate. Then, instruct the students to evaluate each of these viewpoints to generate their own opinion on the topic presented. Have students compare their original opinion of the topic based on prior knowledge and their new opinion based on reading and an examination of various viewpoints.

For example, Ms. Fenway's ninth-grade English students will be debating the value of wearing school uniforms. She begins by having the students read various research on the subject. She asks the students to choose the best article and summarize the author's viewpoint. She leads the students through the remainder of the activity. Gillian's worksheet was completed as follows:

### *Viewpoint Synthesizer*

**Topic:** *Wearing school uniforms*

| The author's viewpoint (summary): | The teacher's viewpoint (summary): |
|---|---|
| *School uniforms are good for students because they reduce school violence. Students don't compete for social status through clothing or accessories. School uniforms also unify the student body because everyone is wearing the same thing.* | *School uniforms help students to focus on school work. When students are wearing the same thing, they can't be distracted by each other's outfits. Self-esteem also improves because students can't make fun of each other if someone isn't wearing the latest "cool" clothing item.* |

| Another source's viewpoint (summary): | A classmate's viewpoint (summary): |
|---|---|
| *School uniforms diminish students' creativity and make them feel trapped. Students need an outlet through which to express their personalities and the best outlet is through their clothing and accessories. Students need sensitivity training so that they diminish the likelihood that they will make fun of someone for being different.* | *I definitely don't think we should have school uniforms. Students have so little power over anything. Especially when students are in middle and high school, they need ways to express their individuality. Students who wear uniforms will be depressed and sullen and learning will not happen.* |

**My viewpoint on the topic:**

*There are pros and cons to the issue of requiring students to wear school uniforms. I think that students have the ability to focus and learn and still be allowed to express their individuality through their own clothing choices.*

## Activity 9: A Scavenger Hunt

Use the chalkboard or overhead to generate a list of everything that the class already knows about the topic to be studied. Then, divide the students into teams, and give each team an identical list of terms and concepts to find in the text. Have the teams preview the text as quickly as possible to find the term/concept and develop a definition or association based on the text. The first team to finish the scavenger hunt wins. Formulate a class discussion in which you compare the information that they found in teams to their initial brainstorming on the chalkboard or overhead.

## Activity 10: Buddy Reading

Divide the students into partners. Discuss with the students the topic or concept about which they will be reading, and possibly allow them to briefly preview the text. Students can compare the amount they know, the depth of their knowledge, and their interest in the topic. After reading, instruct students to identify how the text connected to their prior knowledge. Then, have the students compare which partner found information that most strongly connected to prior knowledge. This discussion will help students learn and retain the new information.

## Activity 11: KWL and KWL Plus

A highly effective strategy, KWL (Ogle, 1986) structures students' thinking before and after reading. Often, it is difficult to begin this activity without building some background knowledge. As a class, complete the "knowledge" portion of the KWL chart. Work with the students to generate questions they have about the topic and complete the center column of the chart. You may want to use this as a previewing activity and have the students' questions result from looking at the headings, subheadings, and pictures associated with the text. Next, have the students read the text. When they are finished, have them record what they learned and any new questions they may have. As an extension, have the students reflect on the importance of the information and how they will use or apply what they have learned to their own lives.

For example, Mr. Ellington's ninth-grade special education geography students are studying climate, in particular what causes local winds. Ariana diligently completes her KWL chart before, during, and after the reading process:

### KWL Chart Plus Reflection

**Topic:** *The causes of local winds*

| Before reading: What do you already know about the topic? | Before reading: What do you want to know about the topic? | After reading: What did you learn? |
|---|---|---|
| *I think wind is caused by warm air moving over cooler air, but I am not sure.*<br><br>*I think some areas get more wind than others depending on how many land features there are such as hills, mountains, streams, lakes, etc. I think living near an ocean can also cause certain kinds of wind.* | *I want to know the difference between storm winds and gentle breezes that you encounter on a typical day. I want to know how destructive kinds of wind can be identified and avoided.* | *Land and sea breezes are caused by an unequal heating of land and water.*<br><br>*Monsoons are winds that change direction from season to season. Mountain and valley breezes are caused by differences in temperature between these two areas.*<br><br>*An anemometer measures wind speed.* |

**Plus: What further questions do you have?** How can you use the information you have learned? What surprised you about the information?

*I am still not sure how dangerous kinds of wind can be avoided. I guess they can't! I think more diagrams in the text would have helped me to better understand exactly how wind is formed. I am not sure if what I learned about how wind is formed matches what I already knew. The author used slightly different words, but I think I already knew the basic concept.*

### Activity 12: Anticipation Guides

An anticipation guide (Thomas & Wilson, 1993) is a list of statements pertaining to a particular topic in a piece of text the students are going to read. Before reading, students determine whether or not the statements are true or false, or whether or not they agree or disagree with them. Students read the text with the intention of confirming their prereading assessment of the statements. After reading, students revisit the statements and identify whether or not the statements are true or false, or whether or not they agree or disagree based on the text information.

To create an anticipation guide, begin by determining the major concepts or themes that you want the students to recognize in the text. Determine the students' prior knowledge of these concepts, and think about whether or not the students have any preconceived beliefs. Create statements about the topic/concepts, and make sure the statement order follows the text. Discuss the statements briefly, and have the students complete their reading following the anticipation guide procedure. Conduct a follow-up discussion in which you focus on the student beliefs that changed or were confirmed.

Mr. Worthington is a 10th-grade English teacher who is collaborating with the 10th-grade history teacher to design a unit in which the students read historical fiction relevant to the historical era that they are currently studying. To begin the unit, students are instructed to complete the following anticipation guide. Completing this guide allows Mr. Worthington to assess the students' prior knowledge and beliefs as well as giving students a preview of some of the themes and concepts that they will be encountering throughout the unit.

### Historical Fiction Anticipation Guide

**Directions:** Before you begin reading the story or novel, complete the "before reading" portion of this anticipation guide. After you have finished reading, complete the "after reading" portion of this anticipation guide.

| Before reading | | Theme | After reading | |
|---|---|---|---|---|
| Agree | Disagree | Historical figures experience the same feelings that I do. | Agree | Disagree |
| Agree | Disagree | Historical figures experience different feelings than I do. | Agree | Disagree |
| Agree | Disagree | Events in history make the people who experience those events feel many things. | Agree | Disagree |
| Agree | Disagree | Authors write historical fiction to help us learn about how people felt about the things that were happening to them. | Agree | Disagree |
| Agree | Disagree | I can relate to other people regardless of the time period in which they lived. | Agree | Disagree |
| Agree | Disagree | I can relate to other people regardless of their race or ethnicity. | Agree | Disagree |
| Agree | Disagree | I can relate to other people regardless of their gender. | Agree | Disagree |

| | | | | |
|---|---|---|---|---|
| Agree | Disagree | I can relate to other people regardless of their beliefs. | Agree | Disagree |
| Agree | Disagree | Historical fiction helps us to develop empathy with people who lived in different time periods. | Agree | Disagree |

**Reflection:** What is the most important theme that you have learned? How does this theme help you to better understand the genre of historical fiction?

## ASSESSING STUDENT MASTERY·OF CONNECTING TO PRIOR KNOWLEDGE

As teachers, we understand the importance of assessing whether or not students have acquired the skill that has been taught. You may choose to use one, many, or all of the activities presented in this chapter to help students become more proficient with connecting text to prior knowledge. As a professional, you will make observations regarding students' acquisition of this skill, but it is also important to formally assess their knowledge and understanding. Here, you will find a generic rubric for assessing the skill of connecting what is read to prior knowledge.

### Prior Knowledge Rubric

Use this rubric to determine students' progress toward mastering the following reading skill: The student relates new information to prior knowledge to better comprehend text.

### *Level 4—Mastery*

- The student makes relevant and insightful connections between the text and personal experience, previously read texts, and/or current events.
- The student modifies existing knowledge based on new concepts encountered in the text.
- The student independently uses strategies to relate new information to prior knowledge.

### *Level 3—Nearing Mastery*

- The student makes some connections between the text and personal experience, previously read texts, and/or current events.
- The student modifies some prior knowledge using the concepts or information found in the text.
- The student uses some strategies to relate new information to prior knowledge.

### *Level 2—Developing*

- The student makes limited connections between the text and personal experience, previously read text, and current events.
- The student attempts to modify prior knowledge based on new concepts encountered in the text.

### *Level 1—Basic*

- The student may or may not be able to make connections between the text and personal experience, previously read texts, and current events.
- The student struggles to modify prior knowledge based on new concepts encountered in the text.

### *Level 0—Below Basic*

- The student makes no attempt to use prior knowledge to make a connection to the text.

# 4

# Understanding Vocabulary Terms and Concepts

## SKILL OVERVIEW

When students can define words in context, their comprehension levels will increase (Johnson & Pearson, 1978; Wittrock, Marks, & Doctorow, 1975). Middle and high school students should be proficient in using context to gain a clear sense of the concept they are exploring, the topics they are studying, and the purpose for their learning. Structured discussions, small-group dialogue, and paired readings will build the students' ability to identify words in context because they will hear their teacher and classmates use unknown words in real-life conversations. When proficient readers encounter a word they do not know, they ask three questions:

1. Do I know this word?

2. If so, how do I know this word? If not, how can I know this word?

3. Do I need to know this word?

Proficient readers answer these questions by using context, activating prior knowledge, and using various resources available to them. Struggling readers have great difficulty using context and will need highly structured word attack strategies to make sense of unknown words.

# SUBSKILLS

## Using Sentence Context to Understand Word Meaning

Students must be exposed to a variety of texts in all content areas. In each subject area, students must be taught how to read the sentences that they encounter to determine word meaning. When using various techniques to make sense of words in sentence context, consider the following word attack strategies:

1. Reread the sentence and try to understand the word based on sentence meaning.

2. Use the dictionary and find a definition that makes sense within the context of the sentence.

3. Reread the previous sentence.

4. Go on and read the next sentence.

5. Ask the teacher or a friend to read the sentence to you.

6. Look for key words in the sentence that may reveal the word's meaning.

7. Stop reading and think about what makes sense.

8. Look for pictures near the word or sentence to see if they help you understand.

9. Think about whether or not you need to know the word. Skip it if you do not need to know.

## Building Awareness of Root Words

One of the main reasons for the exponential gains in vocabulary knowledge in young children is their growing awareness and proficiency with root words, suffixes, and prefixes. Morphology is the ability that students have to use word structures to make meaning of new vocabulary. Explicit instruction that teaches students how to use their prior knowledge to make sense of root words, suffixes, and prefixes will result in growing confidence levels in understanding words and ultimately an increase in reading comprehension. Some key questions will help students with using morphology:

1. What is the root word? What prior knowledge do I have to help me define this word?

2. What is the prefix? What does it mean? How does it change the root word?

3. What is the suffix? What does it mean? How does it change the root word?

4. How does knowing parts of words help me to understand the meaning of new words?

## Interpreting Words With Multiple Meanings

Many words have multiple meanings, and students need to have ways to discern when a vocabulary word that they know does not make sense in the context of the sentence. Often, students will encounter a familiar word being used differently because it has another definition with which they are unfamiliar. It is important to teach students that words are often used differently based on the subject area. For example, in math the word *change* means money. In science, *change* is connected to catalysts and experimentation. In social studies, *change* is connected to politics, history, and economics. A helpful technique to show students the concept of multiple meanings is to create a large comparison chart that shows how many words are used differently in each subject area. Have multiple copies of the chart made so that each teacher can add to the chart as the school year unfolds, showing students how words are used differently across the content areas.

## Using Compare and Contrast to Clarify Word Meanings

Comparing and contrasting is a valuable analytical technique that allows students to explore vocabulary words and their definitions. Students can compare and contrast different roots of words, how the same word is used in different content areas and across contexts, and the relationships between words by solving analogies. Giving students the opportunity to use higher-order thinking skills when exploring vocabulary words and their definitions will help them to better understand the concepts they are learning.

## Identifying Shades of Meaning

When students are able to understand the shades of meaning of vocabulary words, they will have deeper levels of comprehension. The ability to interpret different meanings of vocabulary words is particularly useful when learning key concepts such as conflict, change, freedom, and symmetry. At the middle and high school level, it is particularly beneficial for teachers to plan interdisciplinary lessons in which concepts and key vocabulary are discussed with particular attention paid to shades of meaning. Students will be able to make connections among major concepts but also link facts to the concepts they are learning when they explore multiple meanings.

## Understanding Denotative and Connotative Meanings

By the time students are in high school, it is important for them to know the difference between denotative and connotative meanings. Remind the students that denotative meaning indicates the definition of a term by naming it. Connotative meaning is derived from secondary implications or associated meanings. Being able to connote meaning is a more challenging task because it requires the reader to understand the set of attributes that constitutes the meaning of a term.

### Understanding Words Related to Content Areas and Current Events

Students need to know the technical vocabulary for various content areas to better understand and acquire content knowledge. For example, in science, students should have mastery of certain words, such as *experiment*, *scientific method*, *theory*, *hypothesis*, *catalyst*, and *conclusion*. Proficiency with such content-specific vocabulary will lead to greater facility with learning facts and increase the students' ability to synthesize and evaluate information. It is often helpful to have the students create a word bank or glossary for each of their subject areas so that they can gain facility with content-specific vocabulary.

### Using Dictionaries and Other Reference Materials

Although it is important to teach students how to identify the meanings of words in context and use other text-based strategies, it is also important to give the students continued practice with using dictionaries and other reference materials. Give the students the opportunity to find word meanings by organizing individual and group games such as scavenger hunts. Assign the students some content-specific vocabulary and have them use the guide words at the top of the page to find the word, and then have them identify the word meaning, parts of speech, and root.

## SKILL-BUILDING ACTIVITIES

### Activity 1: Vocabulary Baseball

Games are highly motivational to students, and here is one you may want to try. To set up vocabulary baseball, post a home base, first base, second base, and third base strategically around the classroom. Divide the class into two teams. In addition to 10 batters, each team can have a score keeper and coaches at every base. For the first team up at bat, "pitch" the vocabulary word to the first batter. The batter needs to define the word, use it in a sentence, and spell the word. For each part that the batter does correctly, he or she gets a base. For example, if the batter can do all three things, he or she has hit a triple. When a player cannot do any part, he or she is out. When the team has three outs, it sits down and the other team bats. If the students have prepared for the game, you may not have many outs, so you may have to set a run limit of five runs.

### Activity 2: Double-Entry Journal for Defining Vocabulary

Have the students begin by identifying their purpose for reading. On the left side of the journal, have the students record vocabulary words that are unfamiliar to them. On the right side of the journal, have the students define the words in context and then confirm their definitions by having a class discussion or using the dictionary.

For example, Mr. Manning's eighth-grade language arts students are reading a series of short stories and have been instructed to use the double-entry journal to gather words with which they are unfamiliar. The following is John's journal:

### *Double-Entry Journal for Defining Vocabulary*

**Purpose:** To gather unfamiliar words from the story that I am reading

| Text information | Reader's response |
| --- | --- |
| List words that are unfamiliar to you. | Use a dictionary to define each of the words. |
| *Absurd* | *Making no sense at all, going completely against or having no reason.* |
| *Cherish* | *To feel or show great love for; to value highly; to take special care of.* |
| *Emigrate* | *To leave one's home country or area to live in another.* |
| *Glamour* | *Mysterious charm, beauty or attractiveness* |

## Activity 3: Dramatic Photographs

A great way to build students' understanding of new words is to use drama. Divide students into groups or pairs and have them create a miniskit or dramatic "photograph" that illustrates their understanding of the word. If students created a dramatic photograph of the word *exuberant*, they would have one student with a joyful look on his or her face, frozen in a position with arms outstretched as if to embrace the sun. The other students in the group would be facing the exuberant student in frozen positions with happy looks on their faces.

## Activity 4: Unknown Word Walls

Struggling readers may have difficulty using context clues, so it is important that they be presented with highly structured approaches to making meaning of words through context. Have the students identify unknown words as they read and post these words on sentence strips around the classroom. In their notebooks, have the students record the unknown words, the sentence in which they are used, and an explanation of the context. You may also consider having the students create their own sentences in which the unknown word is used. All students will benefit from this process, but struggling readers will benefit most through the structured support of their teachers and their classmates.

## Activity 5: Attribute Charts

Charting key characteristics is a good technique for identifying attributes related to a particular set of terms. For example, if students were studying mammals in a science class, they would record the mammals in the left-hand column (mice, gorillas, cats, dogs, sheep, elephants, etc.). Across the top of the chart, they would record various characteristics, such as carnivorous, herbivorous, omnivorous, domestic, wild, friendly, not friendly, travels in packs, and travels independently. Students would read the information about the mammals and place a check in the box that corresponds with the particular characteristic that they had confirmed in the text. This technique helps students gain a global understanding of the topic they are studying.

In Mrs. Trubadore's sixth-grade language arts class, students are getting ready to begin a unit on folk literature. Mrs. Trubadore plans to use an attribute chart to introduce key vocabulary terms as well as the important motifs found in classic folklore. She began by introducing the students to the following definition of folktales: Folktales are stories that are passed from generation to generation in the oral tradition. Folklore includes ballads, games, songs, tall tales, legends, epics, fairy tales, myths, old tales, fables, dance rituals, and nursery rhymes. She continued by defining the word *motif* for the students: a recurring theme in literature or art. The following is an example of the attribute chart that she used:

### Attribute Chart

**Topic or concept:** *Folk literature*

| In the columns to the right, please write the titles of the books you read. ⇨  On the lines below, write the list of attributes and continue to check and revise as you continue to read more books in the genre. ⇩ | | | | | | | |
|---|---|---|---|---|---|---|---|
| 1. Unkind parents | | | | | | | |
| 2. Magic—objects, places, and characters | | | | | | | |
| 3. Talking beasts | | | | | | | |
| 4. Tests of the hero/heroine | | | | | | | |
| 5. The quest (search) | | | | | | | |
| 6. Wise women and men (fairy godmothers, witches, and wizards) | | | | | | | |

| | | | | | | |
|---|---|---|---|---|---|---|
| 7. Giants, monsters, and ogres | | | | | | |
| 8. Youngest is often bravest and/or wisest | | | | | | |
| 9. Son and daughter characters | | | | | | |
| 10. Role reversal | | | | | | |

## Activity 6: Personal Connection Vocabulary Strategy

When students make sense of vocabulary words by applying them to their own lives, there is a greater likelihood that they will retain the definitions in their long-term memories. For this strategy, students identify the vocabulary word and draw a simple illustration or symbolic representation of the word. Then, they list their personal associations with the word. For example, if the word is *malcontent*, the students may focus on the word beginning "mal" and associate the word with malicious, malformed, and malignant. Students may notice that all these words have something to do with the idea "bad." After some discussion with a peer group or a buddy over the meaning of the word, students may look up the word in a dictionary. Then, have the students generate a list of examples and nonexamples of the word based on their personal experience.

## Activity 7: Question Cubes

For this strategy, identify the unknown word and have the students use various questions to help them reflect on the usefulness of the word, connections to personal experience, an illustration of the word in action, and where they might encounter the word again. Have the students fold their notebook paper into quadrants to record their brainstorming to each of the previous questions.

To illustrate this activity, let's examine Mr. Brown's application with his sixth-grade language arts class. As students read various texts over the course of a week, they identified words in context that they did not recognize. They recorded the words on their question cubes worksheets, and the following is one of Sarah's vocabulary words:

### *Question Cubes*

| **Identify the unknown word and its definition** | **How does it connect to your personal experience?** |
|---|---|
| *Soothe—to make something that hurts less painful* | *My mom soothes my aches and pains when I am sick. She also soothes my hurt feelings when someone at school is mean.* |
| **Draw a picture of the word:** | **Where might you encounter this word again?** |
| | *I might encounter this word on pain medication or in a story with a character who is hurting.* |

## Activity 8: Cartooning

As the students read, have them make a list of words that they do not understand. After reading, engage students in a discussion in which you identify the most common words not understood and assist the students in defining these words. Provide the students a blank cartoon strip and have them illustrate the five or six key scenes of the book, story, or chapter. Have them incorporate their new understanding of vocabulary words into their cartoons.

## Activity 9: Concept Mapping

Concept mapping is an effective way for students to gain an in-depth understanding of a key concept or topic they are studying. With this strategy, students identify key attributes and details related to the concept or topic. To add variety to this strategy, you could have the students draw pictures or find magazine pictures of the examples and post them around the classroom.

For example, Mr. Lewis's 10th-grade social studies students are studying ancient Rome. In the center of their concept maps, the students would write "Ancient Rome." In each of the surrounding circles, they might write such topics as "gods and goddesses," "fabulous architecture such as famous temples," "definitive social scale with magistrates and important statesmen as well as people who lived in great poverty," and "a massive and well-equipped army."

## Activity 10: Capsule Vocabulary

Originally developed by Crist (1975) and further explained by Irvin (1990), capsule vocabulary incorporates listening, speaking, reading, and writing into the process of learning new vocabulary. Begin by preparing a "capsule" of vocabulary words related to the topic. This capsule could be a real container that holds the words, or you could draw a large picture of a capsule on the chalkboard and "fill" it with the vocabulary words by writing them in the picture representation of the capsule. Next, engage students in an extended discussion in which you use the capsule vocabulary words to discuss the topic. As an extension, you can have the students record the words, have a conversation with a group using the words, listen to the teacher and record the words, write a "ministory" or description using the words, and read the text and record the amount of times the capsule vocabulary words were used. As a variation, have the students write a story after they read and compare the similarities and differences between to their two stories.

For example, Mr. Bloomberg's seventh-grade environmental studies seminar class is learning about the sun's upper atmosphere. He decides to use the capsule vocabulary activity to add some creativity to his seminar. Louann and Mark are partners for this activity, and they created the following capsule activity sheet:

### *Vocabulary Capsule*

**Topic:** *The sun's upper atmosphere*

---

*Chromosphere, kilometers, photosphere, prominences, corona, solar eclipse, sun*

---

**Before reading capsule of key vocabulary:**
**Before reading story or paragraph using the capsule words:**

*There are two layers to the sun's atmosphere: the chromosphere and the photosphere. The corona is at the center of the sun. A solar eclipse happens when the moon passes in front of the sun.*

**After reading story or paragraph using the capsule words:**

*Boy was I wrong! There are three layers that make up the sun's atmosphere: the photosphere, the chromosphere, and the corona. The photosphere is the innermost layer and the chromosphere is the next layer and gives off a weak, red glow that can sometimes be viewed. These flamelike clouds travel away from the chromosphere for thousands of kilometers. They are called prominences and can sometimes be seen during a solar eclipse. The corona is the layer farthest from the sun.*

## Activity 11: Personification Vocabulary

With this strategy, students define unknown vocabulary words and then personify those words. For example, if a student were to personify the word *beautiful*, he or she might write, "Beautiful walks down the street carrying a bundle of roses while flipping her luxurious chestnut-colored hair over her shoulders." If a student were to personify the word *angry*, he or she might write, "Angry likes to hide in old gnarled trees and growl loudly while scratching his head covered with coarse black hair."

## Activity 12: Text Coding

As students are reading, instruct them to use the following codes to mark important text as it relates to examination of vocabulary:

> *?* = Unknown vocabulary word

> ** = Important vocabulary word

> PKV = Prior knowledge vocabulary word

This is a simple but powerful technique that can be used in any content area. You can even provide the students with a chart to keep track of the identified words and then use the chart as a basis for teaching. The headings for the three-column chart would match the text codes: Unknown vocabulary word, Important vocabulary word, and Prior knowledge vocabulary word.

# ASSESSING STUDENT MASTERY OF UNDERSTANDING THE MEANINGS OF UNKNOWN VOCABULARY

As teachers, we understand the importance of assessing whether or not students have acquired the skill that has been taught. You may choose to use one, many, or all of the activities presented in this chapter to help students become more proficient with understanding and integrating new vocabulary.

As a professional, you will make observations regarding students' acquisition of this skill, but it is also important to formally assess their knowledge and understanding. Here, you will find a generic rubric for assessing the skill of vocabulary acquisition.

## Vocabulary in Context Rubric

Use this rubric to determine students' progress toward mastering the following skill: The student understands the use of vocabulary in context.

### Level 4—Mastery

- The student quickly and easily determines the correct word meaning of words found in context.
- The student uses an extensive knowledge of root words to determine the meaning of unknown words in a passage.
- The student interprets words with multiple meanings.
- The student independently uses strategies to understand vocabulary.

### Level 3—Nearing Mastery

- The student determines the correct word meaning of most words found in context.
- The student uses knowledge of root words to determine the meaning of most unknown words in a passage.
- The student interprets most words with multiple meanings.
- The student uses some strategies to understand the use of vocabulary.

### Level 2—Developing

- The student determines some word meanings of words in context when guided by a teacher.
- The student sometimes uses a limited knowledge of root words to determine the meaning of unknown words in a passage.
- The student attempts to interpret words with multiple meanings when guided by a teacher.

### Level 1—Basic

- The student may or may not be able to determine the correct word meaning of words in context.
- The student struggles with using knowledge of root words to determine the meaning of unknown words in a passage.
- The student has difficulty interpreting words with multiple meanings.

### Level 0—Below Basic

- The student makes no attempt to understand the use of vocabulary in context.

# Identifying Significant Information in Text

## SKILL OVERVIEW

When students read, they must be able to quickly identify key concepts to maximize their learning. Previewing the information for text features and skimming and scanning the content can help readers to set the stage for focusing on the facts. Here are some ideas to help the students:

- Demonstrate for the students how to decide if the text should be carefully read or simply skimmed for facts and key information.
- Help the students identify extraneous information.
- Have the students ask questions about information that is confusing or incomplete.
- Instruct students to relate their prior knowledge to the topic.
- Have the students preview the text for content and organizational structure.
- Lead the students through a brief discussion of headings and subheadings. Have them link this information to the facts they already know.
- If the text has many features, such as graphs, charts, and photographs, help the students prioritize their reading.

# SUBSKILLS

## Noticing Text Features

To identify the most significant text information, students must learn to pay particular attention to the following features:

- Headings and subheadings
- Bolded words
- Italicized words
- Captions/labels
- Illustrations
- Photographs
- Charts/maps
- Graphs

## Asking Questions

Model for the students how to ask questions as they read to identify significant text information:

- What are the key concepts and/or main ideas?
- What are the important facts?
- How does the information I am reading connect to what I am learning in class?
- How do the text features help me to understand what is significant?

## Organizing Information

There are many ways for students to organize the information that they encounter. Some of the more traditional approaches include outlining and using note cards. It is important to teach students how to use traditional approaches, but it is also important to show them various techniques to allow for the diverse learning styles in your classroom. These techniques include webbing, double-entry journals, and concept mapping. Given the amount of information that students will interact with over the course of their education, it is essential that they be able to have various tools to sort information into key concepts, main ideas, and supporting details.

## Extracting Appropriate Information

To develop this skill, begin by presenting the students with highly structured "purpose for reading" questions. Have them work in groups to read and answer the questions. Reinforce for the students that they were extracting the information necessary to answer the question. Then, present the students with more general questions and have them practice the skill of extracting the important information. Some questions include

- What is the author's purpose?
- What key information does the author want us to learn?
- What data, facts, or experiences should we gain from the text?
- What are the main ideas and supporting details in the text?
- What important information is included in the text boxes, maps, graphs, and charts?

### Paraphrasing

Being able to restate information in your own words is a critical skill. Begin by having the students preview the text for important information. As they read, have them take notes about information related to the topics or concepts they are studying. Finally, have the students put their notes away and restate the most important information in their own words.

## SKILL-BUILDING ACTIVITIES

### Activity 1: Artistic Creations

To get students started with the skill of summarizing, tell them the definition of *summarizing*: relating the most important information to a given audience. Read students a short piece of nonfiction and tell them to think about the most important information. Then give students a blank sheet of paper and have them draw a picture of the key ideas in the text. Tell them that they can be as creative as they want and that they can use captions or labels, but they are not to write a paragraph. When the students are finished, have them share their artistic creations with the class. Keep track on the overhead or chalkboard of the students' ideas and look for commonalities among their understandings of what is most important.

### Activity 2: Partnered Paraphrasing

This strategy will help the students develop their listening skills as well as their paraphrasing skills. Divide the students into partners. Partner 1 asks a question. Partner 2 answers the question. Partner 1 restates Partner 2's answer. Partner 2 agrees if his or her answer has been correctly answered. The partners switch roles. Here are some sentence starters to help with the paraphrasing:

Let me see if I understand what you are saying . . .

If I hear you correctly, you are identifying . . .

What you are telling me is . . .

### Activity 3: Using Note Cards

Although this strategy is traditional, it is still beneficial to students. Begin by introducing the students to the purpose for using note cards: to have them identify and record significant information in text. When students use note cards, be sure to give them a format to follow so that their information is consistent. Categories that they should include on their note cards include key concept, main idea, supporting details, source, and an evaluation of information.

To illustrate this activity, let's take a closer look Ms. Wolf's recent research project on fossils in her seventh-grade science class. She began by brainstorming various aspects of fossil investigation with the students. Then, she allowed her students to explore a topic of interest and do some independent reading. Students were instructed to take notes using the following note card format. Here's one of Mary's note cards:

> **Key concept:** Fossils — Intelligent mollusks
>
> **Main idea:** Cephalopods are the most advanced form of mollusks and include octopus, squid, and cuttlefish.
>
> **Supporting details:** (1) Cephalopods are active predators which enhances their survival rate. (2) They are very useful fossils for dating rocks.
>
> SOURCE: Taylor, Paul D. (1990). *Intelligent Mollusks. Eyewitness Books: Fossil* (pp. 28-29). New York: Alfred A. Knopf.
>
> **Evaluation of Information:** This information was very useful because it is presented clearly and with lots of pictures, diagrams, and examples. I really understood how important the cephalopods are to the fossil record.

### Activity 4: Put a Box Around What Matters

Have the students read the text, draw a box around what is important, and write a key word or phrase that summarizes the information in the box. If students are not allowed to write in the text, provide them with sticky notes and instruct them to align the note with the text, draw an arrow toward the important information, and write their key word or phrase on the sticky note. As an extension, you can have the students record "boxed" information in the left column of a double-entry journal and write a personal or analytical response in the right-hand column.

Let's examine Mr. Brazelton's 10th-grade history class to understand this approach when identifying key vocabulary. Mr. Brazelton has just begun a unit on the Jefferson era. He introduces the unit by asking the students to identify what they already know about this time frame in history. Then, he asked them to read a portion of their history text and complete the bracketing activity. The following is an example of Mike's worksheet:

### *Put a Box Around What Is Important*

**Topic:** *The Jefferson era*

| Bracketed information and key word | Personal response |
|---|---|
| *(Ensuring that all people have rights)* **Democratic**<br><br>*(Government should play as small a role as possible)* **Laissez-faire**<br><br>*(The Supreme Court has the power to decide whether laws passed by Congress are constitutional)* **Judicial review** | This information is important because . . . I can remember this information by . . . I wonder . . .<br><br>*The word democratic is so important to the history of our nation. I can remember laissez-faire because it reminds me of what has become the mantra of the modern-day Republican party. I wonder what percentage of the time the Supreme Court exercises the judicial review process.* |

## Activity 5: INSERT

INSERT (Vaughn & Estes, 1986) is a more comprehensive notation system that helps readers make decisions as they read as well as evaluate and clarify their understandings of text. Use this system by gradually introducing symbols and by choosing symbols that are appropriate for the text that the students are reading. INSERT will work well as a research strategy.

☺ I agree

X I disagree

+ New information

! Wow

? I wonder

?? I don't understand

!! Important

B Boring

P Pro

C Con

Students may use the ?? notation to signify text they do not understand or vocabulary that they do not understand. This strategy is flexible and may be simplified when necessary. Most important, this strategy makes thinking visible to the students.

## Activity 6: Before/During/After Note Taking

You may want to have students work with a partner to complete this activity. Students can engage in buddy reading in which each student reads a portion of text in a rotating fashion. Introduce students to the reading process in which effective readers make predictions and ask questions before reading, continue to ask questions and make connections during reading, and evaluate their learning after they have read. Provide students with the before/during/after (BDA) checklist for taking notes during the reading process. Guide the students to revisit their BDA checklist frequently throughout reading to remind them of the thinking skills they should be using.

### *A BDA Checklist*

*Planning—Before Reading*

- What do I already know about this topic?
- What interests me about this topic?
- What questions do I have about this topic?
- What do I need to know or do to focus and pay attention to the lecture/ reading?

- What is my purpose for listening/reading?
- How will I be assessed on the information?

### Monitoring—During Reading

- Do I understand what I am hearing/reading?
- Am I organizing the information in the best way?
- What fix-up strategies can I use if I do not understand?

### Evaluating—After Reading

- Did I achieve my listening/reading purpose?
- Can I summarize or paraphrase the information presented in my own words?
- What questions do I still have about the topic?
- Did I use appropriate strategies to help me increase my understanding?
- Do I feel that I understand the material that was presented?
- How can I improve my retention of the material next time?
- What do I have to do next to meet the requirements for the assessment that my teacher has given me?

## Activity 7: Trifold Note Taking

Have the students fold their notebook paper into three sections horizontally. In the first section, have the students preview the headings, subheadings, bolded or italicized words, charts, captions, and diagrams. Have the students make predictions about what they will be reading. Then, have the students take notes about information learned in the center section of their paper. Finally, in the last section, have the students reflect on what they have learned by drawing a picture, writing a personal response, writing a diary entry, or writing an opinion column.

To illustrate trifold note taking, let's look at how Mr. Jones's 10th-grade history class applied this activity to their learning situation. Mr. Jones began by introducing the unit, "Rebuilding the Nation (1864–1877)," and connecting some of the new concepts to the students' prior knowledge. Then, he instructed the students to preview the chapter and use the trifold note-taking worksheet to capture and respond to some of the key text information. Lucinda's worksheet is included here:

### *Trifold Note Taking*

**Topic:** *Reconstruction*

---

**Before reading**

**Describe the headings, subheadings, bolded words, charts, captions, and diagrams.**
*Time lines with world events highlighted; illustrations and pictures on the time line of the Lincoln assassination, the Reconstruction Act, the impeachment of Andrew Johnson, the reelection of Ulysses S. Grant, and the candidacy of Rutherford B. Hayes. Also included are text boxes with chapter points and think-about activities.*

---

**What do you predict you will be learning?**

*I predict that I will learn about Lincoln's plan to reconstruct the South after the Civil War including how to provide aid, medical care, and schooling to the poor and war-stricken people.*

**During reading**

**What are you learning? What surprises, interests, or confuses you?**

I am learning about . . .

- *Help for freed men*
- *Lincoln's assassination*
- *A rebellion in Congress when Republicans refused to let Southern representatives take their seats.*

*It surprises me that it was so difficult to gain support for reconstruction efforts. It also surprises me that security was so poor when President Lincoln was assassinated.*

**After reading**

**Demonstrate your learning by drawing a picture, writing a summary, or writing a diary entry.**

*Dear Diary,*

*I cannot believe how our family was devastated financially and emotionally after the Civil War. We lost all of our materials possessions. But most horrifically, three of my brothers were killed and two others remain missing. I am heartbroken at the cost of this war.*

*Sincerely,*
*Sarah Ruth*
*A Confederate's Daughter*

## Activity 8: Key Word Note Taking

Have the students fold their notebook paper so that they create three columns. Simply have the students record key words in the left column, important details and definitions in the center column, and examples/illustrations in the far right column of the chart. Model for the students how to make inferences by studying the key facts, details, and definitions. After students have completed this note-taking graphic organizer, show them how to use it as a study guide. Model for them how to fold the graphic organizer on the lines that divide the chart. Have the students quiz themselves on the definitions and examples that match the key words. Then, show the students how to turn the study guide over and quiz themselves on key words that match the definitions and examples. Students can work independently to study this information or with a partner. One of the benefits of this technique is that it builds the students' independence in mastering their own learning.

To illustrate this activity, let's look more closely at Mr. Mather's eighth-grade algebra class. Mr. Mather begins by introducing the activity and allowing students to preview the chapter on square roots. Then, he instructs the students to use the key word note-taking worksheet to organize text information. The following is Jerry's worksheet:

### *Key Word Note Taking*

**Topic:** *Square roots*

| Key word | Definition | Examples |
|---|---|---|
| Square roots | If $A = s2$, then $s$ is called a square root of $A$. | $4.5 \times 4.5 = 20.25$ sq. units |
| Radical signs | The symbol for a square root | $2 \times 2 = 4$ |
| Perfect squares | The squares of whole numbers | $3 \times 3 = 9$ <br> $4 \times 4 = 16$ |

## Activity 9: Cornell Notes

Cornell note taking (Pauk & Owens, 2004) is a two-column strategy that has been found to be effective when taking notes on both reading material and class discussion. Follow this step-by-step process to assist the students:

1. Choose reading or lecture material that has a structure based on main ideas and details.

2. Demonstrate for students how to set up the two-column notes. Students should fold their papers approximately 3 inches from the left side of the paper and draw a vertical line in the crease.

3. Demonstrate for the students how to take notes in the larger right-hand column.

4. Divide the students into partners or groups of three or four and have them write a key word or phrase in the left-hand column for each note that they have taken in the right-hand column.

5. Have the students rewrite their notes; reorder or rephrase certain points; add new details; number their subpoints; and add drawings, pictures, diagrams, or charts.

6. Have students rewrite their key words column by clarifying headings, creating symbols, creating acronyms, writing short phrases or questions, and developing any other cues that will help them remember the content in the notes.

7. Students can fold over the right-hand column and refer to the cues to study and memorize the content.

For example, Ms. Mulberry's eighth-grade history class is learning about World War I. She follows the procedures for this activity, and the following is Lindsey's worksheet based on her reading:

### Cornell Notes

**Topic:** *World War I*

| Key words | Definitions and explanations |
|---|---|
| *Nationalism* | *In the 1800s, Nationalists in Europe strove to find more freedom and an opportunity for self-government.* |
| *Militarism* | *The process whereby a nation builds up strong armed forces to prepare for war.* |
| *Mobilize* | *Calling troops together.* |
| *Stalemate* | *Neither warring side is strong enough to defeat the other side.* |
| *Trench warfare* | *Soldiers do not fight openly over land; rather they find retreat in trenches and attack the enemy primarily through shelling.* |
| *Propaganda* | *The policy of spreading particular ideas and beliefs that help one side of the cause and hurt the other side.* |

## Activity 10: Numbered Heads Together Summarizing

Students number off 1 through 4. The teacher gives the teams of four a question and a piece of text. Students put their heads together to read the text and answer the question by focusing on the main idea and supporting details. The teacher calls on number 1's to share their answers. Then, the teams generate a new question for the text. The teacher jigsaws the students by placing the 1's, 2's, 3's, and 4's together to reread the text and answer the new question generated by the previous team.

## Activity 11: Double-Entry Journal for Identifying Significant Information

Have the students begin by identifying the key concept they will be investigating. On the left side of the journal, have the students record important information that connects to the key concept. On the right side of the journal, have the students reflect on important information that they have identified. You can have them write a personal response, ask further questions, or analyze how the author chose to present the information.

For example, Mr. Teller's seventh-grade science class is studying pollution and its effects on the environment. The following is Jamison's double-entry journal reflecting his learning and analysis of the author's effectiveness:

### Double-Entry Journal for Identifying Significant Information

**What is the key concept you are investigating?** *Pollution and its effects on the environment*

| Text information | Reader's response |
|---|---|
| **What important information connects to the key concept? Use headings, subheadings, and bolded words to help you.** | **Did the author choose to present the information in an effective way? Explain.** |
| *Heading:* Pollution—What Is It? | *Yes, the author chose to represent the information effectively. In particular, the photographs are particularly appealing to the reader and emphasize the point that it is important to take care of our natural resources.* |
| *Bolded statement:* The balance in our environment can be upset by the way in which we obtain and use our natural resources. | |
| *Bolded word:* Pollution (the release of substances into the environment that changes the environment for the worse.) | |
| *Two pictures:* One of a barn and cow grazing on open farmland; another of trash under a tree in the woods. | |
| *Caption:* How can such littering be prevented? | |

## ASSESSING STUDENT MASTERY OF IDENTIFYING SIGNIFICANT INFORMATION

As teachers, we understand the importance of assessing whether or not students have acquired the skill that has been taught. You may choose to use one, many, or all of the activities presented in this chapter to help students become more proficient with identifying significant information. As a professional, you will make observations regarding students' acquisition of this skill, but it is also important to formally assess their knowledge and understanding. Here, you will find a generic rubric for assessing the skill of identifying important information in text.

### Identifying Significant Information Rubric

Use this rubric to determine your students' progress toward mastering the following objective: The student can identify the main idea and supporting details in text.

### *Level 4—Mastery*

- The student quickly and accurately identifies the main idea.
- The student identifies the theme in a reading passage.
- The student identifies the supporting details in the text.
- The student applies strategies for finding the main idea and supporting details independently.

## Level 3—Nearing Mastery

- The student identifies the main idea.
- The student identifies the theme in a reading passage with limited guidance from a teacher.
- The student identifies most of the supporting details in the text.
- The student applies some strategies for finding the main idea and supporting details.

## Level 2—Developing

- The student identifies the main idea with some guidance from a teacher.
- The student identifies the theme in a reading passage with much guidance from a teacher.
- The student identifies most of the supporting details in the text with some guidance from a teacher.

## Level 1—Basic

- The student may or may not be able to identify the main idea.
- The student struggles to identify the theme in a reading passage.
- The student identifies some supporting details in the text with much assistance from a teacher.

## Level 0—Below Basic

- The student makes no attempt to identify the main idea and supporting details of informational text.

# 6

## Visualizing Text Information

### SKILL OVERVIEW

As middle and high school students read increasingly complex text, they must be able to visualize the information they encounter. Visualizing (Wilhelm, 1997) is one of the mental building blocks for proficiency in inferencing. Teachers need to be aware that students can use words from text, titles, charts, diagrams, and illustrations to make inferences and thus improve their ability to understand the information. An effective approach to presenting the idea of inferencing is to share with the students some specific descriptions or a scenario and have them make an inference about the events in the scenario. For example, a ninth-grade boy comes home from a football game with a smile on his face. His family can infer that he either won the game or made a very good play offensively or defensively. After presenting students with many such scenarios, their confidence with inferencing will improve.

Next, you can move on to inferencing with text. Share with the students some descriptive scenarios from text that create a visual picture in their minds. For example, the author describes a scene in which the main character is going on a hike in the woods. The teacher can lead the students to "see" the trees, underbrush, birds, trail, and fallen leaves; "hear" the soft whisper of the wind through the trees; and "feel" the slight chill in the air as dusk approaches. Filling in the missing information will help students comprehend textual information. This visualization technique is one that they can transfer across subject areas.

## SUBSKILLS

### Building Visualization Vocabulary

Authors use particular techniques to create images in the reader's mind. These techniques include adjectives, vivid verbs, and figurative language. Reviewing the following terms with students will help them recognize these techniques as they read and eventually incorporate them into their own writing:

**Adjectives** describe nouns.

Example: The *soft* breeze blew through the *budding* dogwood trees as the *glowing* sun set on the horizon.

**Vivid verbs** describe the action of a sentence.

Example: The little girl *jumped*, *skipped*, and *hopped* exuberantly around her father when she found out that she was going to the circus.

*Figurative language* involves using words and phrases to create images in the reader's mind. Figurative is the opposite of literal, which means words that can be taken at their face value. The following are definitions and examples of figurative language terms:

**Alliteration** is the repetition of consonant sounds at the beginnings of words.

Example: Freddy the Fox furiously frowned at Frannie.

**Repetition** is the use of whole words or phrases more than once.

Example: I hear the chirp, chirp, chirp of the robin as the sun beats down, beats down, beats down upon the ground.

**Onomatopoeia** involves using words that sound like things they are describing.

Example: The thunder cracked and boomed in the distance, CRAAACK!

**Hyperbole** is using exaggeration to describe something by stretching the truth in a colorful way.

Example: John Henry hammered through the mountain so fast that the wind was out of breath just trying to catch up to him.

A **simile** uses *like* or *as* to compare one thing to another.

Example: Reading is like riding a roller coaster: full of ups and downs; times when you understand and times when you don't. The key is to hang on because in the end reading, like riding a roller coaster, is such a rush!

A **metaphor** is a comparison in which one thing actually becomes the other.

Example: Reading is a roller coaster: full of ups and downs; times when you understand and times when you don't.

**Personification** is a literary device that gives human traits to objects, ideas, or animals.

Example: The volcano wheezed and coughed before it erupted.

A **cliché** is a tired, overused metaphor or simile.

Example: It's raining cats and dogs.

## Accessing Prior Knowledge

Guided practice with previewing text will help the students to tap into their prior knowledge. Before you have the students begin reading, have them look carefully at the title and identify any visual images associated with the words in the title. Then, have the students preview the text, noting the headings, sub-headings, charts, graphs, and illustrations. Again, have them identify visual images associated with these various text features. It may be helpful to record all these observations on the chalkboard. Finally, have the students make connections between the visual images they have identified and their prior knowledge of the topic. As students read the text, make sure to refer them back to their initial visualizations and ask them to revise or clarify their understandings.

## Analyzing Sensory Detail

Proficient readers use sensory details to make pictures in their minds. These readers are able to use details to see, hear, taste, touch, and smell the images that are described in the text. It is essential for teachers to model how to create pictures in one's mind when reading. Proficient readers create mental images but often do not realize what is going on cognitively for them to "see" the text. Teachers must help proficient readers understand the visualizing skills that they have developed to further build on these skills, and they must help struggling readers to use sensory details to begin the process of visualizing text.

## Creating Mental Images to Remember Details

Retention is a critical component of reading comprehension. As proficient readers enter the text world and begin to form vague pictures of the big ideas, they will also begin to add distinctive impressions of the details. As educators, we often ask students to simply retain the facts, the details, and the small ideas. It is important to teach students that building a strong ability to visualize will help them to retain the big idea(s) and provide the scaffolding on which to hang the details. When we assess students' progress, it is extremely valuable to incorporate many kinds of evaluation. A unit test may include some multiple-choice, true/false, short-answer, and long-answer responses. In addition to the traditional approaches to assessment, make sure to include on your assessment a question that asks the students to reflect on how they used visualization to remember key concepts, facts, and details. Such a component of assessment will help students build their thinking skills and ultimately strengthen their retention of information.

## Creating Mental Images to Draw Conclusions

Drawing conclusions is a skill essential to all subject areas. When students are able to visualize text information, they are better able to understand the relationship among ideas and draw conclusions about the information that they are learning. One strategy that is very useful in helping students with this skill is to provide them with a "purpose for reading" question before reading that requires them to think about the conclusions that they are drawing as they read. Be sure to have the students identify the specific text information that allowed them to draw the conclusion that they did.

## Incorporating New Information

One of the key features of learning and teaching is that new information builds on what is already known. If students gain proficiency with linking new information to what they already know about the topic and making connections across contexts and subject areas, then their learning will improve exponentially. The following are some questions that you can ask students to help them both build their visualizing skills and make connections to incorporate new information into their existing knowledge base:

### Before Reading

- What do you already know about the topic?
- As you preview the text, what images do you see?
- What images do you already have that connect with your current knowledge or understandings of the topic?
- Can you describe these images?
- Can you represent these images either through art or drama?

### During Reading

- What new information are you learning about the topic?
- What images do you associate with this new information?
- Are you visualizing as you read?
- Can you describe these images?
- How do these new images confirm or contradict the images that you identified before you began reading?

### After Reading

- What key information (concepts, topics, and facts) did you learn?
- Have you blended your existing images about the topic with the new images?
- Can you represent the connections you have made between your existing knowledge and new knowledge through art, drama, or writing?

- How does visualizing improve the learning process?
- What strategies did you use to visualize the information you were learning?
- How can you apply these strategies in other content areas?

## Representing Abstract Information as Mental Pictures

One of the most difficult skills is to represent abstract information as a mental picture. For example, if a teacher asks students to read about freedom, he or she may ask students to first identify pictures that come to mind, such as the American flag, the bald eagle, or the Statue of Liberty. As students read, they should be instructed to add to their mental representation by using information from the text.

# SKILL-BUILDING ACTIVITIES

## Activity 1: Newscast

Divide the students into pairs. Have the students assume the roles of news anchors. If the students are reading nonfiction text, have them write new reports as if they are reporting the latest update with regard to the information. If the students are reading historical information or historical fiction, have them research relevant stories of the historical time period of the character. Instruct them to embed stories of the character into the historical stories to dramatize their live newscast. They can conduct interviews and have weather reports, fashion updates, and commercials.

## Activity 2: Asking Questions to Create the Scene

Have the students begin reading text that is visually stimulating. After students have read a few passages, have them stop reading and then discuss or draw pictures related to the following questions:

- What do you see? Hear? Smell? Touch?
- What prior knowledge or experiences do you have that connect with the text?

After reading, continue the questioning to help the students further develop their images of the setting, their relationship to the character, and their relationship to the author.

Imagine the setting from the book/story in your mind:

- Where are you in the setting? Close? Distant? Hiding? Right beside the main character? Above? Below? Behind? Leading the way? Moving or still?
- Are you a confidant? A friend? Connected? Disconnected?
- Which characters do you want to know the best? Why?
- Do you want to help? Give advice?
- Do you want to run far away from the character(s)?
- Where is the author? Is the author close to the character(s)?

### Activity 3: Text Graphing

Text graphing (Lane, 1993) allows the students to visualize the information they are learning as well as evaluate it. This technique is particularly effective to use in social studies class. Have the students list the events that they are encountering in the text. Next, have them think of an artistic representation or symbol for each of the events. Then, present them with the text-graphing template much like the one shown here, and have them evaluate each of the events by drawing their symbols to correspond with the appropriate number on the graph.

***For Example:***

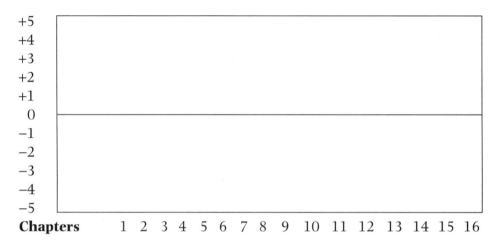

It is important to note that there are not any "right" or "wrong" answers in text graphing, and that students may rate events differently. Students should be encouraged to justify their ratings either in writing or in small-group or whole-group discussions.

- How does the graph prove or disprove our earlier assumptions about the theme?
- At what point on the graph did the character change the most?
- Why did this change occur? What happened?
- Why did the author choose to show the character traits that he or she did?
- How did these character traits affect plot structure?
- What was the author's purpose in this novel? What was the author trying to teach us about human nature?

### Activity 4: Rotating Dramas

Divide the students into partners and instruct them to each take on the role of a different "character" from the text. Then have them interact with each other through dialogue or movement. This interaction should take no longer than 1 or 2 minutes and will create a vivid image in the students' minds regarding the relationships between the people, ideas, or concepts about which they are reading. This technique works across content areas. For example, the characters in social studies may be historical figures or people who live in other countries; the characters in science may be chemicals, elements, or scientific concepts; and the characters in math may be numbers, signs, or symbols.

## Activity 5: Tableau Dramas

A tableau is a frozen scene from the text and is a nonthreatening way to get every student in the class to interact with text. Students need to work with a partner or in groups to create a tableau. Assign each group a portion of text to dramatize. Students work cooperatively to create a frozen scene that depicts the relationship between people, ideas, or concepts from the text. There is no dialogue in a tableau, although students may choose to have their characters engage in a repetitive movement to show some particular feature of the idea or concept they are dramatizing. After the students have created their tableaux, they should perform them in front of the class.

## Activity 6: Talk Shows

Planning a talk show will get the students involved in writing dialogues, developing opinions, and interviewing characters to demonstrate their knowledge of a particular concept or idea. Have the students read the text information and identify the most important points of the text. Then, have the students work with a partner to create a script that illustrates the important points. The talk show host may interview a character or characters, the author, or the reader. Through the interview, the important points of the text must be illustrated. Encourage the students to watch talk shows so that they can assume the demeanor of a talk show host.

## Activity 7: Symbolic Story Representations

Symbolic story representations (Enciso, 1990) involve a technique in which students are given different pieces of colored construction paper and use the paper to tear shapes that represent different ideas, concepts, or characters from the text. Then, the students arrange the shapes on a large piece of construction paper to show the relationships between or among the ideas. Finally, the students explain their creation in small groups or through a written response. The simple act of tearing shapes is highly motivating to students and is a nonthreatening way for them to represent their ideas since little to no artistic ability is required.

## Activity 8: Storyboarding

An essential step in the planning process of movies and TV shows, storyboarding is a great way for students to visualize the sequence of steps in a scientific experiment or the events that unfolded during a particular time in history. Introduce the idea of storyboarding to the students by having them think about a sequence of events or steps with which they are familiar, such as their morning routine before coming to school. Then, have the students read the text and illustrate through symbols and simple illustrations the sequence or steps in the text.

### Activity 9: Four Corners

Middle and high school students greatly benefit from differentiated instruction. Use the four corners of the classroom to focus on different learning styles. Dedicate one corner of the classroom to drama, and label it "The Dramatic Corner." In this corner, provide space for three or four performers and three or four audience members. The Dramatic Corner should have multiple texts, dramatic scenarios, and supplies for making scenery and props. Another corner could be labeled "The Discussion Corner." In this corner, provide materials for four to six students to engage in a discussion about the texts they are reading. This corner should have multiple texts, discussion frames and sentence starters, as well as a tape recorder so that students can tape their discussions and reflect on their communication skills. A third corner could be titled "The Artist's Corner" and provide a rich supply of art materials so that students can create representations of the texts they are reading. The final corner could be titled "The Writer's Corner" and include space and supplies for four to eight writers to reflect on their reading, write poetry, create songs, or write letters that represent key idea and concepts about which they are reading.

### Activity 10: Found Poetry

Ask students to read a story or a chapter in a novel or textbook. Before they read, give them a particular topic, issue, or character to focus on as they read. Ask them to jot down 10 to 15 words or phrases about this topic, issue, or character. Then have them organize the words and phrases into a poem. If you have a small class or a short piece of text, you can photocopy the text and have the students circle the words and phrases as they read and then cut out the "found" words and phrases and mount them on colorful construction paper. This lesson focuses on building the students' strengths in finding significant and relevant text.

To illustrate this activity, let's examine Ms. Lohan's sixth-grade language arts class, which is currently reading Chapter 6, "Harassing Miss Harris," from *The Great Gilly Hopkins* by Katherine Paterson (1978). Ms. Lohan asks the students to focus on the character of Miss Harris, Gilly's teacher, as they read. Ms. Lohan instructs the students to make a list of words and phrases that reveal the character of Miss Harris to the reader. At the conclusion of the chapter, Ms. Lohan helps the students organize their words and phrases into a list poem:

*Found Poem About Miss Harris*

Not

Likely to crumble

Wasn't

Hooked up to other people

Her body totally covered except for

Her eyes

Absolutely just

And absolutely impersonal

Wrapped

In invisible robes

Computer-activated

Brilliant, cold

Totally, absolutely, and maddeningly fair

All her inner workings shinily encased and hidden from view

A flawless, tamperproof machine

Yelling and anger

Underneath the protective garments

## Activity 11: Double-Entry Journal for Analyzing Imagery

Have the students begin by identifying their purpose for reading. On the left side of the journal, have the students record words and phrases that create an image in their minds. On the right side of the journal, have the students identify the senses to which the author is appealing, a personal reflection, and an analysis.

Imagine Ms. Broward's eighth-grade language arts class is reading "All Summer in a Day" by Ray Bradbury (1991). She motivates the students to begin reading by asking them to share a time when they felt completely abandoned, helpless, or alone. She then instructs them to created a double-entry journal on their own lined paper and record images from the text on the left side and write a personal reaction to the text on the right side of the journal. To complete this process, some students may need a very structured set of directions or a series of sentence starters, both of which are included in the Resources. The following is Andrew's double-entry journal:

### Imagery Double-Entry Journal

Title of book, poem, story, or article: *"All Summer in a Day"*

Author's name: *Ray Bradbury*

| Text Information | Readers's Response |
|---|---|
| *Sweet crystal fall of showers* | **Senses:** *Sight and sound* |
| *Concussion of storms* | **Personal reaction:** *I remember when I was growing up in rural Baltimore County and we used to have violent thunderstorms. I must have been nine or ten years old. I remember being fascinated with the storms because my grandfather was also intrigued. We would go stand by the door of the top balcony of the second story of the house and watch the lightning and listen to the thunder. The power would usually go out so there wasn't really anything else to do. But I think that even if there had been electricity, I would have chosen to go watch the storm. However, I can't imagine living with storms every day of my life.* |
| *Drumming gush of waters* | |
| *Thousand crushed forests* | |
| *Gold coin big enough to buy the world* | |
| *Tatting drum of rain* | |
| *Echoing tunnels* | |
| *Clear bead necklace of rain* | |
| *Tidal waves* | |
| *Gushing rain* | |

*(Continued)*

(Continued)

| Text Information | Readers's Response |
|---|---|
| | *I would have been sad like Margot, too, if I never got to see the sun.*<br><br>**Analytical reaction:** *The author is doing an excellent job using metaphors to make a picture in my mind. I especially like the image of the "clear bead necklace of rain." It leaves me with a picture of the beauty and symmetry of rain. This image contrasts with the horror of living with the darkness of rain every day, like the children in the story have to do.* |

SOURCE: List of images from Bradbury (1991, p. 7).

## Activity 12: Bookmarking

This strategy is a great way for students to keep track of text-based information at the same time they are applying their knowledge of content vocabulary. Simply introduce a purpose for reading, such as identifying specific techniques that the author uses to create a picture in the reader's mind. Then, have the students record specific examples of particular techniques on the front of their bookmarks. Instruct the students to refer to the content vocabulary listed on the back of their bookmarks as needed.

| Front of Bookmark | Back of Bookmark |
|---|---|
| As you read this book, you will be recording examples of imagery on this bookmark. On the line under pg. and par., record a brief notation to yourself about the passage. You will be responding in detail to these passages in your double-entry journal.<br><br>pg. _____ par._____<br>_____<br><br>pg. _____ par._____<br>_____<br><br>pg. _____ par._____<br>_____<br><br>pg. _____ par._____<br>_____<br><br>pg. _____ par._____<br>_____ | Imagery is defined as "artistic" words, phrases, and passages that create a mental picture in the reader's mind. Literary devices that authors use to create pictures in the reader's mind include:<br>    Adjectives<br>    Vivid action verbs<br>    Figurative language<br><br>Figurative language tools include:<br>    Similes<br>    Metaphors<br>    Personification<br>    Onomatopoeia<br>    Hyperbole<br><br>Adjectives and sensory details might include:<br>    Colors (be aware of negative and<br>        positive connotations)<br>    Dark vs. light<br>    Shapes and sizes |

## Activity 13: Double-Entry Journal for Analyzing Characters

As an adaptation, have the students record words and phrases or passages that create a picture of the character in their minds on the left side of the journal. On the right side, have the students make an inference about the character traits of the character, write a personal reaction, and write an analysis.

Mr. Cooper's sixth-grade language arts class is reading *The Great Gilly Hopkins* by Katherine Paterson (1978). The following is Annemarie's double-entry journal analyzing the character of Gilly:

### Character Double-Entry Journal

Title of book, poem, story, or article: <u>The Great Gilly Hopkins</u>

Author's name: <u>Katherine Paterson</u>

| Text Information | Reader's's Response |
|---|---|
| *In her new foster home, Gilly Hopkins makes mean faces at the other foster child named William Earnest (W.E.) in order to intimidate him. Her faces resemble Godzilla and Count Dracula. W.E. quickly disappears behind Maime Trotter, Gilly, and W.E.'s foster mother.* | **Character traits:** *Mean, intimidating*<br><br>**Personal reaction:** *I remember when I was in the fourth grade and I rode the bus to elementary school. There was a boy who rode the bus named Michael. He was the meanest kid on the bus. One day he threw another kid's shoes out the window. Another day, he stole a kid's homework and never gave it back. I remember sitting still in my seat and hoping that he wouldn't pick on me next. I don't think he ever did. I remember my bus driver yelling a lot, but never doing anything significant to stop the terrorism. If Gilly had ridden my bus back then, I would have dealt with her the same way I did Michael. Sit still, be quiet, and hope she doesn't see me. I am glad I have changed and am now able to confront bullies, even if they're adults!*<br><br>**Analytical response:** *The author does a good job comparing Gilly to Count Dracula and Godzilla. I immediately get a picture in my head of Gilly's body and a weird combination of Dracula and Godzilla's head resting on her body. The image is almost comical. It causes me to question whether she is really that scary and to wonder what made her put on a mean, harsh exterior. I also like the author's comparison of W.E.'s disappearance to a toothpaste lid disappearing down a sink drain. This comparison was very effective because it showed me how quickly W.E.'s head disappeared. The author used the comparison to relay the information instead of telling me directly. This made the event in the story more interesting and vivid.* |

SOURCE: Summary of Paterson (1978, p. 6, par. 1).

### Activity 14: Text Coding

Having students code text helps them increase their comprehension during reading. Begin by refreshing students' memories about the five senses. Share with them the five codes to use for identifying images that appeal to the five senses (an eye for sight, a nose for smell, an ear for sound, a tongue for taste, and a hand for touch). Find a short piece of descriptive text; make an overhead transparency; and, using an overhead marker, use the appropriate code to mark words, phrases, or sentences that appeal to particular senses. Instruct them to read a piece of text, code for sensory detail, and then use the worksheet to respond to the sensory images that they identified. Other possible codes include

CT = character trait

CPA = character physical appearance

## ASSESSING STUDENT MASTERY OF VISUALIZING TEXT INFORMATION

As teachers, we understand the importance of assessing whether or not students have acquired the skill that has been taught. You may choose to use one, many, or all of the activities presented in this chapter to help students become more proficient with visualizing information in text. As a professional, you will make observations regarding students' acquisition of this skill, but it is also important to formally assess their knowledge and understanding. Here, you will find a generic rubric for assessing the skill of visualizing key images and concepts as you read.

### Visualization Rubric

Use this rubric to determine your students' progress toward mastering the following objective: The student uses visualizing strategies to comprehend text.

### *Level 4—Mastery*

- The student combines prior knowledge with text information to create visual images in his or her mind.
- The student uses sensory details to create images and make meaning of text.
- The student independently uses visualization strategies to comprehend text.

### *Level 3—Nearing Mastery*

- The student combines prior knowledge with text information to create some visual images in his or her mind.
- The student uses some sensory details to create images and make meaning of text.
- The student uses some visualization strategies to enhance comprehension.

### *Level 2—Developing*

- The student combines some prior knowledge with text information to create visual images in his or her mind with guidance from a teacher.
- The student uses some sensory detail to make meaning of text with guidance from a teacher.

### *Level 1—Basic*

- The student may or may not be able to combine prior knowledge with text information to create visual images in his or her mind.
- The student visualizes the details in the text with much assistance from a teacher.

### *Level 0—Below Basic*

- The student makes no attempt to use visualizing strategies to enhance comprehension.

# Asking Questions to Develop a Deeper Understanding

## SKILL OVERVIEW

Questions are particularly motivating to middle and high school students because they are at a point in their lives where they want to understand and make sense of the world. With regard to reading, questioning strategies can help arouse curiosity, provide direction for research, formulate a purpose for reading, and stimulate further reading and investigation about a topic.

In an educational climate driven by assessment and accountability, it is important to understand the difference between assessment questions and genuine learning questions. Typical assessment questions are those questions that we already know the answer to and that we use to measure the academic achievement of students. Genuine learning questions are those questions that we do not know the answers to, arouse our curiosity, and require further inquiry on the part of both the teacher and the student. There is a place in the classroom for both kinds of questions, and it is essential that students become proficient at using reading strategies that allow them to answer both kinds of questions accurately, elaborately, and with confidence.

# SUBSKILLS

## Categorizing Questions

When students are able to categorize the kinds of questions they are being asked, they are better able to understand their purpose for reading. Understanding and applying such strategies as the Question/Answer Relationships strategy (described later) can assist readers in knowing the kinds of reading and thinking they have to do to proficiently answer a question. The skill of categorizing is one that is useful both in school and in various real-world contexts. When applied to reading and questioning, make sure to point out to the students that the categorizing skill is highly valuable and integral to success in many life situations.

## Monitoring Comprehension

When teachers model reading strategies, it is important that they know how to gradually release the responsibility to the students. Students must have access to a variety of strategies to clarify, revise, and reformulate their initial understandings of text content. There are two types of explicit modeling that can ensure that students move toward taking responsibility for monitoring their reading comprehension: talk-alouds and think-alouds (Davey, 1983). In a talk-aloud, present the students with the components of a particular monitoring strategy and then orally lead them through these steps by questioning and showing the students how to apply the strategy to a particular piece of text. It is particular useful to make an overhead transparency of the text and the steps of the strategy to share with the students. As you lead the students through the strategy, appropriately mark the text on the overhead to demonstrate exactly how to apply the strategy.

Think-alouds require the teacher to present the steps of the strategy and then share with the students the actual thinking that accompanies use of this strategy. Teachers should make their own confusion, misconceptions, general wonderings, and discovery apparent to the students. It is important to show the students that you as an adult reader also have to wonder, clarify, and question to come to an understanding of text information.

## Organizing Content Knowledge

Students need to have a variety of techniques for acquiring content knowledge. To do this, teachers should consider focusing instruction on key concepts. The following are some basic questions that you can ask yourself when planning a unit:

1. What is the major concept being investigated or studied?

2. What are the guiding questions that will help the students make sense of this topic?

3. What texts will I use to help the students find answers to the guiding questions?

4. How will I help the students organize the information that they find to maximize their content knowledge and its connections to the major concept?

## Accessing Prior Knowledge

Students must access their prior knowledge to construct meaning. The following is a step-by-step process for connecting prior knowledge to the content learned during daily instruction. Post these questions on a chart or on the chalkboard to help guide students throughout their learning experiences in your classroom:

- What do I already know about the topic?
- How does the text connect to what I know?
- How does the connection further my understanding of the topic?

## Inferencing

Students will need to be adept at inferencing to make sense of complex text. Well-developed inferencing skills allow the students to connect their prior knowledge to the text and comprehend the information at much deeper levels. The following are some questions that students can ask themselves to build inferencing skills:

1. How do I interpret this information?

2. What are my observations after looking at headings, subheadings, and pictures?

3. How does my prior knowledge help me to make reasonable inferences?

## Asking Questions to Seek Elaboration and Clarification

Students must be able to clarify and elaborate on their initial understandings of text. To access deeper levels of meaning in the text, it is important for the students to be able to ask themselves questions such as the following:

1. What is the information teaching me about the topic?

2. What is the author's message?

3. How do the details enrich my understanding of the main concept?

# SKILL-BUILDING ACTIVITIES

## Activity 1: Trivial Pursuit and Brain Quest

Divide students into teams and ask general questions from such games as Trivial Pursuit and Brain Quest. Allow students 1 day to research various topics of interest and generate their own questions that can be used for cooperative games to answer knowledge-based questions. Gradually incorporate questions from concepts that students are learning in your classroom, and require students to make inferences and extend their thinking.

Imagine that Mr. Wellington's 12th-grade history class is learning about the 13 English colonies. He begins by asking questions from Trivial Pursuit to motivate the students. Then, he asks the students to generate their own Trivial Pursuit questions to be used in a class game to review the concepts from the colonial period in American history. The following is Allison's worksheet with information gathered from reading and research:

### Trivial Pursuit

**Topic:** *13 Colonies in American history*

| Concept | Question | Answer | Inference required? (Yes/no) |
|---------|----------|--------|------------------------------|
| *Puritans in Massachusetts* | *What is a Puritan?* | *Puritans wanted to separate from the English church and desired simpler forms of worship.* | *No* |
| *The New York Colony* | *What is a patroon?* | *Owners of huge estates or manors who promised to settle at least 50 European farm families.* | *No* |
| *The New Jersey Colony* | *What is a proprietary colony?* | *The king gave the land to proprietors who divided the land, rented it, and made laws for the colony.* | *No* |
| *Pennsylvania* | *Why was William Penn's family surprised?* | *He joined the Quaker religion which was hated by many people. Quakers refused to fight in wars and were actively vocal against war.* | *Yes* |

## Activity 2: Partners Question

Students write three questions on a slip of paper using their class notes and information from the text. Divide the students into partners, and each partner asks a question while the other partner answers. Students can compile the questions and answers in a graphic organizer such as the one shown here. This strategy helps students review material before a quiz, develop listening skills, and check for understanding during a lesson or unit.

For example, Ms. Elsworth's ninth-grade science class is studying the geologic timescale. She asks the students to do reading and research to generate a study guide for their unit. The following is James and Steven's worksheet:

### *Partners Question*

**Topic:** *The geologic timescale*

| Questions | Answers |
|---|---|
| **Partner #1 question:** *What are trilobites?* | *Animals that lived in the oceans about 600 million years ago.* |
| **Partner #2 question:** *What is the geologic timescale?* | *A history of the earth based on observations of rocks and fossils.* |
| **Partner #1 question:** *What are eras?* | *Time intervals or five periods of time that divide the geologic timescale.* |
| **Partner #2 question:** *What are the names of the eras?* | *Cenozoic, Mesozoic, Paleozoic, Proterozoic, and Archeozoic* |
| **Partner #1 question:** *What are periods in time?* | *Smaller intervals of time that some eras of the geologic time-scale are divided into.* |
| **Partner #2 question:** *What are epochs?* | *Even smaller intervals of time that divide recent periods of the geologic timescale.* |

## Activity 3: Question Webs

Question webs are a great way for students to gather a lot of information about one question. These questions can be student or teacher generated. Students record their question in the center of the web. Then, they read and research the answers to the question by accessing a variety of resources. It is particularly motivating to students if they can work as a team to gather the information to answer the question at the center of the web. After they have gathered enough information, they work together to synthesize what they have learned into a coherent response. Students will need you to model the synthesis of information gained. Have a sample question web on large butcher paper, and then use two highlighters to code essential and extraneous information. Demonstrate for the students how to blend, combine, and connect the essential information into a response to the question.

## Activity 4: Bloom's Taxonomy Questioning

Use the following chart to help students generate questions at increasingly higher levels of complexity.

| Thinking skill | Key words | Sample directive |
|---|---|---|
| Knowledge: Recall information. | Define, describe, identify, label, recall, state, select | Label the following diagram. |
| Comprehension: Understand the meaning of information. | Defend, explain, distinguish, extend, interpret, predict, summarize, recognize | Explain the relationship between _____ and _____. |

*(Continued)*

(Continued)

| Thinking skill | Key words | Sample directive |
|---|---|---|
| Application: Use a concept in a new situation. | Apply, change, compute, demonstrate, discover, modify, prepare, produce, show | Demonstrate your knowledge of _____ by drawing a picture. |
| Analysis: Separate concepts into parts so that structure may be understood. | Analyze, break down, compare, contrast, diagram, deconstruct, differentiate, distinguish, outline | Outline the information about _____ to show your understanding. |
| Synthesis: Put parts together to form a whole. | Categorize, combine, compile, compose, devise, reconstruct, reorganize, revise, rewrite | Compose an essay showing your understanding of _____. |
| Evaluation: Make judgments about the value of ideas. | Conclude, critique, defend, describe, evaluate, interpret, justify, relate, support | Justify your conclusion about _____. |

### Activity 5: Strategy Questioning

In addition to teaching students how to ask questions about text information, it is also important to teach students how to ask questions about the best strategies to use to help them acquire knowledge. Use the following questions to guide the students in developing this skill:

*Questions for thinking about a strategic approach:*

- What parts of the text are difficult or confusing?
- What parts of the text are boring?
- What strategies can you use to make the text interesting?
- What strategies can you use to better understand the text?

*Questions for understanding the process of reading:*

- What new information did you learn about reading?
- How can you apply your knowledge to reading other texts?
- Why is a strategic approach to reading important?
- What advice can you give to other readers about the process of reading?

### Activity 6: An Archaeological Dig

Have students begin by listing random, unconnected questions about a given topic. As their reading and questioning skills improve, encourage them to build their questions so that each answer creates a deeper understanding of the topic or concept under investigation. Provide further structure by having the students record significant text information on the left side of the chart and reflecting on the text information by responding to the sentence starters on the right side of the chart.

Let's examine Mr. Forrester's ninth-grade history class, which is currently studying the Kennedy era in American history. Mr. Forrester structured this activity to allow students to take maximum ownership for their learning. The following is Mandy's worksheet with information gathered after reading and research:

### An Archaeological Dig

**Topic:** *The Kennedy era*

---

**Before reading questions**

*Why was this time period so turbulent?*

*What goals did Presidents Kennedy and Johnson have for the nation?*

*Why was Kennedy assassinated?*

---

| During reading questions | Responses |
|---|---|
| • *What were the economic and social policies that most affected the nation?*<br><br>• *Why did racial discrimination exist during this time frame?* | • I was confused when . . .<br>• I want to understand the information about . . . because . . .<br>• I wonder if . . .<br>• When I continue reading, I most want to know about . . .<br><br>*I wonder why Congress did not support President Kennedy's poverty programs designed to help 39 million Americans.* |

---

**After reading synthesis:**

*The 1960s and '70s were years of turmoil for the American nation. Both Presidents Kennedy and Johnson made efforts to make life easier for poor people and to eliminate racial discrimination. Some believe that Kennedy was assassinated for his efforts to improve the life of the average American.*

---

### Activity 7: More Coding for Quality Questioning

Coding text (Harvey & Goudvis, 2000) is highly useful during reading to ensure that students engage with the information as they are reading. You can create codes simply by thinking of the topics, concepts, or ideas that you want the students to reflect on and then assigning a single letter to represent each idea. A particularly powerful set of codes includes the following: text-to-self (T-S), text-to-text (T-T), and text-to-current events (T-CE). Readers will consciously make note as they are reading of times when the text connects to their own lives, to another text, and to information related to the world. Students can write the codes directly on the text or on sticky notes.

### Activity 8: Concept and Fact Questions

Provide the students with two kinds of sticky notes: concept and fact. Instruct them to read the text information and record questions that require inferencing, reference to concept knowledge, connections to other texts or information learned, or further research on the large sticky notes. Essentially, the students are capturing the "big" ideas on the concept sticky notes. Instruct the students to record fact-based questions, right-there questions, and questions about vocabulary on the little sticky notes, which are intended to represent smaller ideas. After reading, create a T chart on the chalkboard labeled "Concept Questions" on the left side and "Fact Questions" on the right side. Students place their sticky notes on in the appropriate column. Discuss whether or not the questions are "correct" in that they do represent conceptual or factual information. Allow the students to come back up to the board and choose a sticky note to which they will respond either orally or in writing.

### Activity 9: I Wonder . . . Poems

After you have presented a topic or concept to the students, have them work in groups to write a "I wonder . . . poem." Instruct students to simply record all their questions about the topic by beginning with the stanza starter "I wonder . . . ." Post the poems around the classroom and have the students refer to them throughout learning of the new topic or concept.

### Activity 10: Double-Entry Journal for Asking Questions

Have the students begin by identifying their purpose for reading. On the left side of the journal, have the students generate questions that must be answered to achieve their purpose for reading. On the right side of the journal, have the students answer the questions asked as they read.

For example, Mrs. Emerald's sixth-grade social studies class is learning about an era in Roman history known as the "twilight of Rome." Students complete reading and research from various sources to complete the activity. The following is Maryanne's double-entry journal:

**Double–Entry Journal for Asking Questions**

**Topic:** *The twilight of Rome*

| Text information | Reader's response |
|---|---|
| Generate questions that you have about the topic you will be studying. | As you read, record the answers to your questions. Does the author do a good job answering your questions? Explain. |
| *Why did the "twilight" of Rome occur?* | *There was economic chaos and frequent civil wars. Christianity arose and paganism declined.* |
| *Why did the West decline?* | *German people entered the city in droves, Rome was sacked, and the last emperor lost power in 476 A.D.* |
| *Why did the East survive?* | *Known as the Byzantine Empire, the heavily populated and wealthy East survived until 1453 A.D.* |

## Activity 11: Text Coding

As students are reading, instruct them to use the following codes to mark important text as it relates to their purpose for reading:

*???* = I don't understand this concept.

*??* = I don't understand this sentence.

*?* = I don't understand this vocabulary word.

PK? = I am not sure how this information connects to my prior knowledge.

Another simple strategy for using text coding across the curriculum, this particular adaptation can be used in a variety of ways to get students to think critically about text. If students are allowed to write in the text, you can have them use one, all, or a combination of these codes to identify questions about what they are learning. If students are not allowed to write in the text, you can provide them with Post-it notes to mark the text as they read and then instruct them to make a list of questions on their own lined paper.

## Activity 12: Question/Answer Relationships

Question/Answer Relationships (QAR) is a reading strategy that requires the reader to think about the relationship between the text and the question that he or she needs to answer. QAR develops the inferencing skills of the reader.

Answers to questions may be found in four places:

1. Right there: Details that are literal and are easy for the reader to find.

2. Think and search: Details are located throughout the text, and the reader must be able to search through the text and keep the question in mind at the same time.

3. On my own: Students must access prior knowledge about the topic and about reading, make inferences, make connections between the text and prior knowledge, and make connections between the texts and other texts.

4. Author and me: Students must access prior knowledge about being an author to understand the choices and decisions of the author.

### A Quick 10-Step QAR Lesson Idea

1. Select appropriate text for the students to read on a particular topic or theme.

2. Decide on a purpose for reading—What is it you want the students to know and understand after their reading?

3. Design questions that lead the students to this knowledge and understanding.

4. Make sure you have a combination of different QAR questions.

5. Present the students with the purpose for reading.

6. Present them with the questions they need to read. Help the students identify a key word in the question that will help focus their reading. They may even want to write the focus words on their bookmarks in the space provided.

7. Identify the thinking skills necessary to answer each question.

8. Allow students to read the material silently and use the bookmark to identify text that will help them answer the questions.

9. After the students have finished reading, model for the students how to respond to each question and how to find the text to support their responses.

10. Repeat the lesson with new text and allow the students to go through the process independently.

## QAR Bookmarks

| **Front of Bookmark** | **Back of Bookmark** |
|---|---|
| As you read this text, you will be recording examples of important information needed to answer your questions. On the line under pg. and par., record a brief notation to yourself about the passage. Remember to think about the question/answer relationship.<br><br>pg._____ par._____<br>_____<br><br>pg._____ par._____<br>_____<br><br>pg._____ par._____<br>_____<br><br>pg._____ par._____<br>_____<br><br>pg._____ par._____<br>_____<br><br>pg._____ par._____<br>_____ | Purpose for reading:<br>_____<br><br>Key words in reading questions:<br><br>1. _____<br>2. _____<br>3. _____<br><br>1. **Right there:** Details are literal and easy for the reader to find.<br><br>2. **Think and search:** Details are located throughout the text and the reader must be able to search the text for the answer(s) to the question.<br><br>3. **On my own:** The reader must access prior knowledge about the topic and reading, make inferences, make connections between the text and prior knowledge, <u>and</u> make connections between the text and other texts.<br><br>4. **Author and me:** The reader must access prior knowledge about being an author in order to understand the choices and decisions of the author. |

# ASSESSING STUDENT MASTERY OF ASKING QUESTIONS TO GAIN UNDERSTANDING

As teachers, we understand the importance of assessing whether or not students have acquired the skill that has been taught. You may choose to use one, many, or all of the activities presented in this chapter to help students become more proficient with asking questions throughout the reading process to better understand the text information. As a professional, you will make observations regarding students' acquisition of this skill, but it is also important to formally assess their knowledge and understanding. Here, you will find a generic rubric for assessing the skill of asking key questions to gain a better understanding of the key concepts and topics presented in the text.

## Questioning Rubric

Use this rubric to determine your students' progress toward mastering the following objective: The student uses questioning strategies to comprehend text.

### Level 4—Mastery

- The student organizes text information to thoroughly answer a specific question about the text.
- The student asks questions before, during, and after reading or listening to text.
- The student independently uses questioning strategies.

### Level 3—Nearing Mastery

- The student organizes most text information to answer a specific question about the text.
- The student asks some questions before, during, and after reading or listening to text.
- The student uses some questioning strategies with limited guidance from a teacher.

### Level 2—Developing

- The student organizes text information to answer a specific question about the text with much guidance from a teacher.
- The student asks some questions before, during, and after reading or listening to text with much guidance from a teacher.

### *Level 1—Basic*

- The student may or may not be able to organize text information to answer a specific question about the text.
- The student asks limited questions before, during, and after reading or listening to text.

### *Level 0—Below Basic*

- The student makes no attempt to use questioning strategies to promote comprehension.

# Drawing Conclusions and Making Inferences

## SKILL OVERVIEW

Many middle and high school readers will know how to link text to what they know. Teachers will need to explicitly teach questioning skills, however, for struggling readers to know how to raise questions and find answers. In addition, proficient readers will need to have guided practice to strengthen their existing questioning skills. When readers ask questions such as "How does my prior knowledge help me to understand the text?" and "How does using my visualization techniques help me to create a complete picture of what's going on in the text?" their ability to make inferences develops.

## SUBSKILLS

### Making Interpretations

When students make interpretations about text meaning, they are tapping into higher-order thinking skills. Questioning, visualizing, and inferencing are developmental processes that aid readers in deepening their interpretations of the text. Proficient readers will examine cause-effect relationships, compare and contrast information, and engage in problem-solving techniques to gain more from the text than what is merely on the page.

## Making Speculations

Speculating about future events in the text, implications for the reader, and the importance of text information helps readers to build the foundation for drawing conclusions and inferencing. When students wonder about the text, they

- Create mental images to develop a clearer picture of the text.
- Link personal experience and prior knowledge to the text.
- Develop deeper levels of comprehension.
- Gain an increased appreciation for reading.

## Linking Prior Knowledge and Personal Experience

Whereas proficient readers react to text in a variety of ways, struggling readers do not have a mental "toolbox" from which to respond to text by inferencing and drawing conclusions. Students need to be explicitly taught how to identify important text information, choose a method for reacting, and link prior knowledge and personal experience to the text.

## Making Observations

Proficient readers make observations about text features, text content, and the author's choices. Insightful observations provide the groundwork for conclusions and inferences. For example, when a reader can identify specific aspects of a text feature, the likelihood of making critical inferences about the connection between the text feature and the author's purpose is greatly increased. Some ways to increase the students' observational skills include teaching students how to

- Skim and scan for specific text features or specific content.
- Read silently and generate questions.
- Read with a buddy and generate questions.
- Pause during reading to respond, react, and reflect.
- Reread for clarification.

## Identifying and Assessing Evidence

One of the most effective ways to teach students to identify and assess evidence is to present them with a question; require them to read to answer the question; require them to gather text evidence to support the answer to the question; and, finally, show them how to assess the validity of the information, the credibility of the sources, and whether or not the information is comprehensive enough to answer the question.

## Interpreting Nonfiction Text

Some readers believe that nonfiction text simply contains information to be learned. It is important to convey to students the importance of interpreting nonfiction text and dispel the notion that the information is simply to be acquired. Students need to be able to evaluate the author's message, understand how their beliefs and attitudes about the topic are being shaped, and connect the text information with what they have already learned about the topic.

## Predicting Outcomes

To make meaning of text, students need to be able to predict the overall meaning of the text and how they will use the text once they are finished reading. As students read, they need to be able to draw inferences and thereby predict outcomes. For example, if students are reading about the Louisiana Purchase in social studies class, they need to know how this event connects to the concept of Manifest Destiny. By drawing inferences about events in history, events in stories, or concepts in science class, students will be able to predict what it is that they will need to do with the information once they are finished reading.

## Conveying Underlying Meanings

It is important that middle school readers be able to both identify and convey the underlying meaning in text. Often, authors weave their bias throughout the text in such subtle ways that it is difficult for even the most astute reader to identify the author's intention. The following questions will help the students identify the underlying meaning in the text:

- What does the author believe about the topic? How do you know?
- What does the author want you to learn from this article?

Give students multiple opportunities to convey text meanings to other students. Also provide the students with opportunities to generate their own expository writing and evaluate it for underlying meaning.

## Using Explicit and Implicit Information

Middle and high school students must be taught how to identify the explicit text information and how to draw conclusions about the implicit text information. One of the most valuable ways to get the students to understand implicit information is to have them identify the text that is not there. What did the author choose to leave out? Why? These questions will bring students closer to identifying implicit information.

## Making, Confirming, and Revising Predictions

Before students read, they must be able to make predictions about the information they are about to learn. To do this, they need to preview the text and infer what the author wants them to learn. As the students read, they need to think about their earlier predictions for the purpose of confirming or contradicting their initial thinking. As they continue the process of reading and when they are finished reading, they need to be prompted to revisit and revise their earlier predictions and examine how the author was shaping the information to create their final understanding of the text.

# SKILL-BUILDING ACTIVITIES

## Activity 1: Inferencing About the Author

Begin by having the students read the text and identify important events. Instruct the students to record specific, relevant text information on the left side of a double-entry journal format. Have the students use the right side of the double-entry journal to reflect on what the author wants them to learn, what the author believes about the subject, and whether or not they share the author's beliefs. Helpful sentence starters include

The author wants me to learn . . .

The author believes . . .

I do/do not share the author's beliefs because . . .

## Activity 2: Text as Words/Text as Mind Images

One of the goals of sound reading instruction is that students understand that the words on the page do not hold all the meaning of the text. Have them use a double-entry journal format to record the specific information from the text on the left and the "text as images" on the right side of the journal. Students must learn that the text in their head is a compilation of all the prior knowledge and personal experiences that they bring to their reading experiences. Encourage the students to draw pictures or create symbols to represent the text in their minds.

For example, Mr. Lennar's seventh-grade science class is doing an "Undersea Life" unit and preparing for a dissection lab. To tap their background knowledge, Mr. Lennar has the students read about squid. The following is Jeremy's worksheet in which he identifies key facts from the text that he reads and draws a picture on the right side to make sense of his newly acquired knowledge:

### *Text as Words or Images*

**Topic:** *Undersea life*

| Text as words (in your own words) | Text as images (from your own mind) |
|---|---|
| *A giant squid has eight arms. Baby giant squids are 25 feet in length and weigh 200 lbs. They have tentacles. The biggest giant squid may be as long as 60 feet and weigh more than a ton. They are not often observable because they swim very deep, maybe as deep as 3,000 feet. Squid have suckers that are used to capture prey. These suckers have tiny teeth.* | *25 ft.* <br> *Baby squid* |

## Activity 3: Talking Responses

Providing students with a talking response system can be a highly effective way for them to keep track of important text information that they would like to revisit. Have the students "talk through" a response to text with a partner. You might have them to use a text-coding strategy to guide their talking responses. Simply have them record text information that corresponds with the coding that they used to mark the text. Then, have the students demonstrate through a talking response the ability to infer, predict, draw a conclusion, question, or make connections to prior knowledge.

## Activity 4: Guiding Questions

Using concept-based principles is the most highly effective way to help students retain factual information. Make sure to identify the concept that you want the students to learn throughout the course of the unit. Present the students with guiding questions that will help them to categorize and make sense of the vast amounts of information they will be learning.

## Activity 5: Inferencing Cubes

Have students divide their notebook paper into quadrants to make inferences about the people, events, settings, and other important facts in the text. Instruct the students to make a connection to the concept being studied and the guiding questions they are investigating. Consider dividing the students into groups of four and having each partner take the responsibility for one of the boxes in the inferencing cubes.

For example, Ms. Everly's 11th-grade U.S. history class is studying the Boston Massacre to determine its importance in our nation's history. She arranges the students in groups of four and distributes a note card to each student. Each student in the group is responsible for a different set of information from the reading: people, events, settings, or important events. At the conclusion of information gathering, the students are instructed to make an inference about the importance of what they have learned. The following is a worksheet completed by Alex, Patrick, Julio, and Adam:

### *Inferencing Cubes*

**Topic:** *The Boston Massacre*

| People | Events |
|---|---|
| *Angry colonists, British soldiers* <br> *Crispus Attucks, black sailor in Sons of Liberty* <br> *Sam Adams* <br> *John Adams, lawyer* | *Angry colonists yell insults at British soldiers.* <br> *The soldiers fired into the crowd and killed five people including Crispus Attucks.* <br> *Sam Adams's writings further inflamed the colonists.* <br> *John Adams defended the soldiers for their actions.* |

*(Continued)*

(Continued)

| Settings (time and place) | Other important facts |
|---|---|
| *Boston Commons House*<br>*March 5, 1770* | *The Townshend Acts were repealed the same day as the Boston Massacre. The colonists were happy about this action and peace returned to the colonies for a few years.* |

### Inference (Why is this information important?)

*The most important part of this information is that John Adams defended the soldiers and was determined to give them a fair trial. This idea of a fair trial is one of the tenets that our country is founded on. So easily, the soldiers could have been seen as murderers without any rights and consequently been executed.*

## Activity 6: Postage Stamps

Begin by providing students with a purpose for reading. You may want to remind them of the concept they are studying and refer them back to guiding questions. Have students record significant text information and their own inferences about the text. Then, have the students discuss their observations with a partner and record his or her inferences. Give students an opportunity to read about the topic from another source and make an inference. Finally, have the students design a postage stamp that illustrates the inference they have made about the text.

## Activity 7: Colored-Pencil Revisions

Have students fill out graphic organizers about the setting or character in their stories. Have them draw pictures of the settings or characters or both in their stories. With a different colored pen or pencil, have them add to their graphic organizers based on their pictures. If students are reading the same novel, have them share pictures with students in their group and continue to add to their graphic organizers with a different colored pen.

Discuss with students the inferences they made as artists. Have them add the number of inferences in their pictures. Remind them that an inference is when their brain logically fills in a missing piece or aspect of the story (could pertain to character, setting, or plot).

## Activity 8: Postcard Predictions

Have students read expository or narrative text. Require them to pause in their reading after they have gained enough information to be able to respond in a meaningful way. Have them identify the most important points in the text through a summarization or paraphrasing activity. Then, have them draw a conclusion about the author's purpose. Based on the author's purpose, have them identify what will happen next in the text. Instruct the students to convert their prediction into a postcard to a classmate in which they draw a picture that represents the most important points of the text on the front and reveals their prediction through the message on the back.

## Activity 9: Exit Passes

Before reading, review with the students the concept being learned and the guiding questions. Preview the text by asking students about the text features and their possible connections to the topic and concept they are learning. As the students are reading, have them record their observations about the text features in the text. Then, have them make inferences about the text features' connections to the major concept being studied. Have them write their inference on an "exit pass" that they submit at the end of the class period.

To illustrate this activity, let's look at Mr. Hampton's eighth-grade language arts class, which is beginning a community service project. The class has been instructed to choose an important issue and write letters to the editor about the issue. After examining data, the class determined that it wants to tackle the issue of bicycle helmet law. The class does a lot of research, and the following is Leonard's exit pass regarding text features and resulting inferences that he made:

---

**Exit Pass**

*After looking at the map insert of the United States and the embedded key, I see that almost half the states have a law or are working on getting one. I infer that the author wants me to think about the laws in my own state. The insert photograph of a young boy putting on his helmet is probably supposed to inspire readers to put on their helmets.*

---

### Activity 10: Concept Portraits

Have the students draw an illustration of the concept or topic. You will find that the students will combine the information from the text and the "text in their heads" to create an illustration. Instruct the students to reflect on their illustration and make observations about the details, colors, and ideas that were from their prior knowledge about the topic.

### Activity 11: Double-Entry Journal for Drawing Conclusions

Have the students begin by identifying their purpose for reading. On the left side of the journal, have the students record information that matches their purpose for reading. On the right side of the journal, have the students draw conclusions or make inferences.

For example, Ms. Jensen's 12th-grade astronomy seminar is studying meteor storms. To prepare students for some examination of the night sky, students have been instructed to read about meteor showers and meteoroids. The following is an example of Jolene's worksheet that she completed while doing her reading and research:

### *Double-Entry Journal for Drawing Conclusions*

**Purpose for reading:** To gather information about meteors, meteoroids, and meteor showers

| Text information | Reader's response |
|---|---|
| What information from the text matches your purpose for reading?<br><br>*In 1833, many fast-moving balls of fire streaked across the sky.*<br>*Because people didn't know much about meteors back then, they tried to reach into the sky and catch a "flying light."*<br>*Today scientists can predict when meteor storms will occur.*<br>*Burning meteoroids are called meteors.*<br>*Meteoroids can travel through space at 160,000 miles an hour.*<br>*Meteors are sometimes called shooting stars but they are not.*<br>*When a comet travels near the sun, the heat causes pieces to come off. These tiny pieces are called meteoroids.* | What conclusion can you draw about the concept you are studying? What conclusion can you draw about the author?<br><br>*Modern scientists have learned a lot about meteors, meteoroids, and meteor showers. Because "action" in the night sky is beautiful, it causes people to wonder and want to know more.*<br>*The author is very excited and interested in meteors and meteoroids. He uses headings and subheadings to show his belief that the night sky is exciting entertainment: "Nature's Fireworks" and "The Century's Last Big Show."* |

# ASSESSING STUDENT MASTERY OF DRAWING CONCLUSIONS AND MAKING INFERENCES

As teachers, we understand the importance of assessing whether or not students have acquired the skill that has been taught. You may choose to use one, many, or all of the activities presented in this chapter to help students become more proficient with drawing conclusions and making inferences. As a professional, you will make observations regarding students' acquisition of this skill, but it is also important to formally assess their knowledge and understanding. Here, you will find a generic rubric for assessing the skill of drawing conclusions and making inferences to understand the deeper meaning presented in the text.

## Drawing Conclusions and Making Inferences Rubric

Use this rubric to determine your students' progress toward mastering the following objective: The student draws conclusions and makes inferences about text information.

### Level 4—Mastery

- The student thoroughly interprets text information to make inferences.
- The student draws insightful and relevant conclusions about text information.
- The student uses strategies to independently draw conclusions and make inferences.

### Level 3—Nearing Mastery

- The student interprets some text information to make inferences about text information.
- The student draws some relevant conclusions about text information.
- The student uses some strategies to draw conclusions and make inferences.

### Level 2—Developing

- The student interprets some text information with support from a teacher to make inferences about text information.
- The student draws some relevant conclusions with support from a teacher about text information.

### Level 1—Basic

- The student speculates in a limited manner about text meaning to make inferences and draw conclusions.

- The student reacts to the text by drawing on limited personal experience or prior knowledge that may be irrelevant or unconnected.

### *Level 0—Below Basic*

- The student makes no attempt to draw conclusions or make inferences about nonfiction text.

# 9

## Analyzing Text Structure

### SKILL OVERVIEW

Using different structures allows authors to organize and present information in ways that meet the needs of the intended audience. Well-written text will reflect unity and coherence because the ideas will be organized and the relationships between and among ideas will be made clear to the reader. However, students often encounter poorly presented text in which the ideas are not presented clearly and the relationships between or among ideas are vague, disorganized, or nonexistent. If students understand how structural patterns are used, they will be able to make sense of well-written text easily. In addition, if students encounter poorly organized text, they will know why the information seems inaccessible and be able to analyze the text by using their knowledge of structural patterns.

Text structures can be identified through the use of certain structure words. Knowing how to identify text structure helps readers to be able to remember text information better. Also, when readers understand how authors use text structure, their writing skills improve because they have a better understanding of how to organize text to achieve their own purposes for writing.

### Text Structure Chart

| Text structure | Definition | Key structure words |
|---|---|---|
| Description | Author gives examples and details to better describe a topic. | For example, for instance, specifically, in addition |

(Continued)

| Text structure | Definition | Key structure words |
|---|---|---|
| Sequence/narrative | Author writes the main idea and details in a specific order. Examples: chronological; order of importance. | First, second, third, then, next, another, additionally, at last, in conclusion, before, after, later, in the beginning, in the end |
| Cause/effect | Author presents a topic or issue and shows the relationship between the causes and effects related to the topic or issue. | If, then; consequently; because, then; as a result; therefore |
| Comparison/contrast | Author presents a topic or issue and shows the similarities and differences between subtopics related to the topic. | Similarly, on the other hand, but, by contrast, in the same manner, as opposed to |
| Problem/solution | Author presents a problem and provides a solution often through argument. | However, therefore, in addition |

It is important to note that some texts are a combination of structures. Sometimes there are structures within structures.

## SUBSKILLS

### Identifying Text Structure

When authors want to show a sequence of events, ideas, or steps, they will use narrative or sequential order as a text structure. Often, sequential text in social studies will tell the story of a war, the life of a historical figure, the signing of a treaty, or the demise of a civilization. Sequential text in science will outline the steps of an experiment. In math, sequential text will describe the steps of a particular problem-solving process. Teachers must demonstrate to the students how to identify sequential order and how to apply this structural approach to their own writing.

### Evaluating Compare and Contrast Structure

To show the similarities and differences between or among various topics or ideas, authors often will use a compare and contrast structural pattern. Compare and contrast may involve an element of analysis because the writer may include an evaluation of which method, approach, or idea is the best. Astute readers need to be aware of how their feelings about the topic are being shaped.

### Examining Cause and Effect Relationships

When the author wants to show the relationship between events and consequences, he or she will often choose a cause/effect structure. Often, there is a discernable if/then pattern that the reader will be able to recognize. It is important to teach students that although causes have related effects, there is often a slightly more complicated element to this structure in which the effects are often the "cause" of a new problem that has a new "effect." Cause/effect structures show readers the relationship between ideas and events. Critical readers should be taught how to assess when a writer is making illogical leaps and attempting to assign a cause/effect relationship without adequate support.

### Assessing Problem/Solution/Support Structure

When texts are arranged in a problem and support structure, the writer introduces a particular issue or problem, offers a solution, and builds support for the solution. For example, the writer may propose building a community center. Support for this idea may include the following: (a) A community center will get members of the community involved and interacting with each other in a positive way; (b) more people engaged positively will reduce crime; and (c) if the community center includes support for students, their grades will go up and member of the community will have more hopeful futures. The problem/solution/support structure is very useful for persuasive pieces of writing, including editorials.

### Recognizing Bias in Problem/Solution Structure

A problem/solution/support structure is one of the most common organizational structures in persuasive writing. Writers may include the pros and cons for the solution. This approach relies heavily on persuasive techniques because the writer often has a particular solution in mind and will craft the text to prove his or her solution. Critical readers need to be taught how to recognize bias and how to evaluate whether or not an argument is balanced.

## SKILL-BUILDING ACTIVITIES

### Activity 1: Simple Prediction Skits

A common structure that students will encounter, particularly when reading stories, is the narrative or sequence structure. Instead of discussing predictions, have students assume character roles and act out their predictions about future events in the story. Allow the students an opportunity to plan their skits by giving them a graphic organizer to plan out a logical sequence of events based on what they have experienced so far in the story.

For example, Mr. Emory's sixth-grade language arts class is reading the novel *Hatchet* by Gary Paulsen (1987). Students have been instructed to write a short skit to dramatize the most important parts of Chapter 1. The following is Jimmy and Robert's worksheet. To avoid using lots of class time performing skits, have students perform their minidramas in small groups and then perform a few of the strongest skits for the entire class. Have the students record the commonalities among skits.

## Sequence Planner for Skit

**Partners:** *Jimmy and Robert*
**Purpose:** *To draw conclusions about the most important parts of Chapter 1.*

---

**Characters:**

*Brian Robeson, 13 years old*

*Pilot, mid-40s*

---

**Setting:**

*Depart from Hampton, New York*

*Flying over endless, green northern wilderness*

---

**Sequence planner:**

| |
|---|
| **Event #1:** *Brian arrives at a small airport to fly in a single-engine plane. He sits in the copilot's seat and the flight is exciting at first.* |
| **Event #2:** *Brian starts thinking about his parents' ugly divorce. He feels burning tears but does not cry.* |
| **Event #3:** *The pilot begins to talk to Brian and encourages him to manage the controls briefly.* |
| **Event #4:** *Brian remembers that his mom gave him a hatchet to wear on his belt for the plane trip. He thinks more about the divorce.* |
| **Event #5:** *The pilot has a massive heart attack and Brian finds himself alone in a flying plane with a pilot who is either dead or in a coma.* |

**Prediction about next event:** *Brian will land the plane by himself and find himself in the wilderness. The pilot will wake up and help him survive. The hatchet will also help him.*

**Performance notes:** *Jimmy will play Brian frantically trying to fly the plane. Robert will play the comatose pilot who will wake up once Brian has landed the plane. They will make a plan as to how to survive in the wilderness.*

## Activity 2: Cause/Effect Dramatic Responses

Provide the students with situations from the text. Then, present students with the if/then construct for thinking about relationships between events or ideas in text. Have the students create dramatic responses to text that illustrate cause/effect. For example, if the main character steals money from another character, that event is a "cause" for a variety of possible effects. The violated character may retaliate, the main character may repent for stealing, another character may catch the main character and confront him or her, or the violated character may understand the main character's transgression and offer to help. Students can act out these possibilities and then read to confirm or contradict their dramatic prediction.

Imagine Ms. Tully's sixth-grade language arts class is reading *The Great Gilly Hopkins* by Katherine Paterson (1978). After reading the first chapter, Louise's worksheet had the following information. Keep in mind that Louise and three other classmates talked about and dramatized their prediction before they summarized it on their worksheet.

| Summary of dramatic prediction (What will happen next?) | Confirmation or contradiction based on text |
| --- | --- |
| *Gilly's new foster mother, Maime Trotter, will get mad at her in the next chapter and yell at her. Gilly will continue to do mean and unpredictable things.* | *While it's true that Gilly continues to have obnoxious behavior, like not combing her hair, Maime Trotter does not get mad at her or reprimand her in any way.* |

### *Dramatic Predictions*

**Event:** *Gilly enters her new foster mother's home and bangs on the piano and dusts the piano bench with a sofa cushion.*

## Activity 3: Calendar Page Predictions

Have students pause in their reading of a story. Provide them with a blank calendar page and have them plan out a month in the life of the character based on the information so far in the text. Have the students work with a partner to describe why they chose the particular sequence of events for their calendars. Make the connection for the students that it takes inferencing skills to predict a logical sequence of events based on the information provided in the text.

## Activity 4: Cause/Effect Study Skills Analysis

Provide the students with a variety of scenarios connected to school and study skills. The scenarios should be both positive and negative. For example, Johnny does not study for his science quiz scheduled for Friday, Suzy works very hard to write her story for language arts class, and Steven does all his math homework for 1 month. Present these scenarios as the "cause" of a cause/effect relationship. Ask the students to brainstorm two logical effects for each of the scenarios. Be sure to have the students read cause/effect text and apply their knowledge of these relationships to their reading.

### Cause/Effect Relationships

**Negative scenario**
**Topic:** *Studying*

| Cause | Effect |
|---|---|
| *Johnny doesn't study for his science quiz scheduled for Friday.* | *He fails the science quiz by earning a 55%.* |
| *He fails the science quiz by earning a 55%.* | *His parents are very angry with him and take away several privileges.* |

**Positive scenario**
**Topic:** *Studying*

| Cause | Effect |
|---|---|
| *Suzy works very hard to write her story for language arts class.* | *She earns an A on her paper.* |
| *Suzy earns an A on her paper.* | *She feels very proud, and the paper is published in the school newspaper.* |

## Activity 5: Silly If/Then Chain Reactions

Direct the students to arrange their chairs in a large circle. Start the chain reaction by creating an if/then statement, such as "If I go to the mall, I know that I will get an ice cream cone." Have the next student continue by stating, "If I get an ice cream cone, I know I will . . . ." The chain reaction of statements will continue around the circle. Students will have a lot of fun with this activity. Finally, have them identify if/then relationships in text.

## Activity 6: Letter Writing and Community Activism

Identify with the students many ways that they could positively impact their school or neighborhood communities. Have them read a variety of local newspaper articles related to community issues. Inform the students that they will be writing letters to real audiences intended to solve a community issue or problem. Have them plan their letters by identifying real audiences, targeting problems that impact those audiences, and brainstorming solutions for the problems.

## Activity 7: Problem/Solution Games

At the end of a unit of study either in history class or with regard to a literature theme, generate a list of problems that were encountered. Have the students study the problem list and know the solutions or outcomes to each of the problems. Divide the class into two teams and have each team select a representative. Serve as the game show host and ask the representatives to come to the front of the class. Present the representatives with a problem from the text. To get a point for their team, the representatives must identify the context of the problem and the solution or outcome as it was presented in the text. Have teams choose different representatives for each problem so that the maximum number of students get to participate.

## Activity 8: Super Sequence Chains

Provide the students with various topics and have them write one sentence about each topic. Then have them pass their paper to the next student and add the next event. Encourage the students to vary their transitions and not just use *next* and *then*. Have the students continue passing papers for approximately 15 minutes. Stop and have some of the students share. Ask them about the quality of the stories and whether or not adding more information would in fact improve their narratives. Remind the students that authors need to be judicious when adding events to stories.

As an adaptation, give the students several simple topics or "how-to" ideas and have them complete a sequence chain. Topics may include brushing your teeth, making a sandwich, and making an ice-cream sundae. Encourage students to be as detailed and specific as possible. After they share their how-to creations with the class, have the students read sequential text and recall or identify the steps or events with great detail and precision.

## Activity 9: Transition Word Puzzles

Divide the students into groups and give them small segments of text in which the transition words have been deleted. Have the students identify the correct transition words for various pieces of text and then identify the text structure based on the transition words. Finally, have the students write a rationale for why the author chose a particular text structure to achieve his or her purpose. Have the students share their rationales with a partner.

## Activity 10: Double-Entry
## Journal for Analyzing Text Structure

Have the students begin by identifying their purpose for reading. On the left side of the journal, have the students record organizational text features and key words and phrases from the text that illustrate text structure. On the right side of the journal, have the students identify the text structure and evaluate the author's use of structure and how it helps or hinders students in achieving their purpose for reading.

Before beginning this activity, remind the students of many of the common text structures and encourage them to make notes to themselves as they read about the structures being used. Possible codes to simplify their note taking include

C/C = Compare/contrast

C/E = Cause/effect

P/S = Problem/solution

D = Descriptive

N = Narrative

When applying this strategy, it is important to focus the students on the author's purpose for using a particular structure. For example, Mr. Allington's 11th-grade U.S. government class is learning about the beginnings of the federal court system. To fully explore this concept, students will be reading the historical context for this important development in U.S. history, particularly with regard to Washington's presidency. The following is Adam's text structure analysis:

### *Analyzing Text Structure: Double-Entry Journal*

**Topic:** *George Washington as president*
**Purpose for reading:** *To determine and analyze text structure*

| Text information | Reader's response |
|---|---|
| What key words and organizational techniques can help you identify the text structure? | Did the author select the best structure for sharing the information? Explain. Did the text structure help you to achieve your purpose for reading? Explain. |
| *Colorful time line with dates and pictures beginning with 1789 (Washington's inauguration) and ending with 1801 (Jefferson becomes the third president).* | *Yes, the author chose the best structure which is narrative to explain the time line of events before and after the creation of the federal court system.* |
| *Headings:*<br>*President Washington*<br>*Hamilton and the National Debt*<br>*Opposition to Hamilton's Plan*<br>*Strengthening the Economy*<br>*The Whiskey Rebellion* | *Yes, I achieved my purpose for reading and the text features (time line and headings) made that easy to do.* |

## ASSESSING STUDENT MASTERY OF ANALYZING TEXT STRUCTURE

As teachers, we understand the importance of assessing whether or not students have acquired the skill that has been taught. You may choose to use one, many, or all of the activities presented in this chapter to help students become more proficient with analyzing the different forms of text structure that authors use. As a professional, you will make observations regarding students' acquisition of this skill, but it is also important to formally assess their knowledge and understanding. Here, you will find a generic rubric for assessing the skill of analyzing text structure and its affect on readers.

**Analyzing Text Structure Rubric**

Use this rubric to determine your students' progress toward mastering the following objective: The student understands the use of text structures in various texts.

### Level 4—Mastery

- The student recognizes and analyzes text structures in a variety of texts.
- The student evaluates the author's purpose when choosing various forms of text structure to affect the reader in a particular way.
- The student independently uses strategies to understand structural patterns and organization in informational texts.

### Level 3—Nearing Mastery

- The student recognizes and analyzes most text structures in a variety of texts.
- The student evaluates the author's purpose when choosing various forms of text structure to affect the reader in a particular way with limited guidance from a teacher.
- The student uses some reading strategies to understand structural patterns and organization in informational texts.

### Level 2—Developing

- The student recognizes and analyzes some text structures in a variety of texts with some guidance from a teacher.
- The student makes some attempt to evaluate the author's purpose when choosing various forms of text structure with guidance from a teacher.

### Level 1—Basic

- The student has limited ability to recognize text structures.
- The student struggles to understand why authors choose particular text structures to achieve their writing purpose.

### Level 0—Below Basic

- The student makes no attempt to understand structural patterns and organization in informational texts.

# Evaluating the Author's Viewpoint

## SKILL OVERVIEW

All students must be able to understand the relationship between the reader and the author. Being able to identify an author's viewpoint is a reading skill essential for building the deepest levels of text comprehension. Building a mental picture of the author helps readers to understand the author's choice of topic, text structure, and language. When middle and high school readers are able to understand the author's choices, they will also be able to critique the author's style and identify strengths and weaknesses in word choice and organizational structure. Ultimately, students will be able to conceive of themselves as creators of text and apply their critical skills to their own writing to meet the needs of their intended audience.

## SUBSKILLS

### Understanding the Difference Between Fact and Opinion

When reading in the content areas, middle and high school students will encounter various forms of expository text, and they must understand how authors use fact and opinion to achieve their purpose. Authors write for many purposes: to inform, to persuade, to express personal ideas, to teach, and to entertain. When they choose their examples and supporting details particularly in informational and persuasive writing, authors use a combination of facts and opinions. It is important for readers to be able to distinguish between facts and opinions so that they can sort the text into information that they should retain about the topic and information that is the viewpoint of the author. This skill of distinguishing between fact and opinion is essential if middle and high school students are going to evaluate the integrity of the author. Readers should know that authors sometimes attempt to disguise opinions as facts to be more persuasive. Critical readers will be able to recognize when they are being manipulated and think about the text in terms of the credibility of the author.

## Understanding the Author's Word Choices

When presenting informational text, authors should use calm, precise, controlled language. The words in the text should reflect a logical author who is knowledgeable about the topic and intent on informing or teaching the reader about the topic. Good informational writers use rhetorical questions, incorporate figurative language when appropriate, and vary their sentence length and structure. Most authors not only want the information to be accessible but also want to achieve their purpose by allowing the reader to access the text comfortably by making the word choice and language interesting, compelling, and appropriate to the audience's knowledge level, age, and experiences.

## Evaluating Sentence Structure and Text Structure

Stylistic choices regarding sentence structure also make text information more accessible to readers. Varying sentence structure and length is a technique that authors use to make their ideas flow smoothly. In addition, middle and high school readers need to understand that information should be presented in an organizational structure that is appropriate to the author's purpose. Authors use description, cause/effect, compare/contrast, problem/solution, proposition/support, and sequence to present information. Text structure provides a framework for readers to learn the information, and proficient readers will recognize the structure that the author is using and anticipate how the information will unfold. When authors appropriately use language structure, they build their credibility in the reader's mind. Readers assume that if authors are skilled at presenting the information, they are also knowledgeable about the topic.

## Determining Author's Viewpoint Through Context

Sometimes it is valuable for students to do some extra research to understand the author's viewpoint. Understanding that there is a context from which the author's viewpoint was created can greatly enhance text comprehension. Questions that will help determine the context include

1. When and where did the events in the article take place?

2. What are some current events connected to the topic?

3. What is the author's connection to the topic?

Sometimes context is irrelevant or difficult to determine. When working with many different kinds of text, it may be challenging to get information about the author and his or her connection to the topic. When appropriate, however, provide students with information about the author and his or her connection to the topic and any other outside information relevant to the topic.

### Identifying Methods Used to Convey Viewpoint

There are many methods that authors use to convey their views on a topic: personal experience stories, facts and statistics, and expert opinions from various sources. Again, critical readers need to know when such techniques are being used so that they can determine whether or not the information they are reading is biased or fairly presented. The following questions may help your students evaluate the methods that the author used to convey viewpoint:

- How did the author introduce the topic? Was this approach effective?
- How did the author use an organizational structure to achieve his or her purpose?
- Did the author use an appropriate balance of facts and opinions?
- Is the author's bias toward the topic apparent?
- What information should the author have added?
- What information could the author delete?
- What questions do you have for the author?

## SKILL-BUILDING ACTIVITIES

### Activity 1: Talk Show Interview

Divide the students into partners and assign one student the role of talk show interviewer and the other student the role of the author. After reading the text together either silently or as alternating oral readers, have the students work together to generate questions that the talk show host will ask the author. Have the students discuss possible answers. Allow partners to perform their question/answer sessions for the whole class. Require students to identify any insights they gained about the author's choices by participating in this activity.

### Activity 2: Character Bags

As students are reading a story or novel, have them record information about their character. The following miniprompts may help students gather necessary information:

1. Age and gender of main character:

2. Physical traits of main character:

3. Three character traits of main character:

4. Setting(s) of your book:

5. Family of the main character:

6. Main character's interests or hobbies:

7. Most important events to the main character:

After students use these prompts for brainstorming, have them create a bag as if it was owned by the character. It may be a purse, a book bag, a suitcase, a briefcase, or a duffel bag. Instruct the students to include 8 to 10 items. After students have created their bags, have them write a rationale for the items they chose to include and analyze how they used the author's viewpoint to select each of the items.

### Activity 3: My Opinion/the Author's Opinion

Have the students read text that contains a combination of facts and opinions. Provide students with a three-column chart that has three categories: facts from the text, the author's opinion of the topic, and my opinion of the topic. Have the students complete the chart, and then discuss with them the differences between fact and opinion as well as the similarities and differences between their opinions and the author's opinions.

Imagine Ms. Donald's ninth-grade science is studying astronomy. To get students thinking critically about the topic, she exposes them to many articles about planets and the universe. The following is Julie's worksheet:

### *My Opinion/the Author's Opinion*

**Topic:** *The universe*
**Purpose:** *To distinguish between the author's and reader's opinion on a topic*

| Facts from the text | The author's opinion of the topic | The reader's opinion of the topic |
|---|---|---|
| *Two scientists discovered planets that could possibly support life.* | *The author is excited about this possibility because she uses exclamation points to state the facts.* | *I think it would be cool if scientists found other planets where we could possibly live.* |
| *Finding new planets should get easier as we create new technology.* | *The author thinks new technology is great because she states that she is looking forward to seeing how the technology is used.* | *I think technology is great and allows us to do and find many things that we couldn't do without it.* |
| *There may be other intelligent life besides us in the universe.* | *The author says, "Can't wait to meet the aliens" and even though this is funny, I believe the author really means it.* | *I think I would be scared to meet aliens. I am happy here on Earth but like reading about the universe.* |

## Activity 4: Biased and Nonbiased Storytelling

Have students sit in a large circle. Begin by telling two simple stories about your morning. The first version of the story should include language that is calm, reasonable, and nonbiased. Present the facts only in an objective manner. The second version of the story should include similar information but should include emotional, biased judgments about the events of your morning. Then give the students a topic such as "our school cafeteria" or "a recent sporting event." For students who are independent, you can have them generate their own topics from personal experience.

Involve all students by having them take turns telling one nonbiased sentence about the topic they have chosen. Then, have them go around again and tell one sentence that is overly emotional and judgmental. Discuss with the students how important it is for them to use reasonable, rationale language and examples when presenting information to prove their credibility as writers. Have students read text that has nonbiased language and analyze the author's choices in presenting his or her viewpoint.

## Activity 5: Author Portraits

Have the students create a representation of the author by drawing his or her head and shoulders. Then, instruct the students to create "thought bubbles" around the author's head that contain the opinions of the author on the topic. Guiding questions may include

- What does the author hope to accomplish through his or her writing?
- What action (if any) does the author want the reader to take?
- What does the author believe about the setting in the article/story?
- What does the author believe about the people in the article/story?
- What does the author believe about the issues described in the article/story?

Instruct the students to give the author a facial expression that represents his or her beliefs about the topic and fill in the thought bubbles with statements that reflect answers to the guiding questions.

## Activity 6: Dramatic Inferencing

Again arrange the students in a large circle and have them take turns reading the same piece of text. Divide students into partnership and instruct them to assume roles that represent the most important characters about which they have read. Have the students create short skits that illustrate scenes or dialogues that must have taken place in the story but the author chose not to write about. After they perform their skits, have the students write explanations that show their understanding of the choices that authors make regarding information to include and not include in the text.

## Activity 7: Author on Trial

To complete this activity, you as the teacher will take on the role of the author. Divide the class in half. Have one half of the class work with a partner to prove that you (the author) presented your ideas in a balanced and nonbiased manner. Students will have to find specific examples from the text to prove their point and generate questions that will help you (the author) show that you presented the information fairly. The other half of the class will work with a partner to prove that you (the author) did not present your ideas in a balanced manner. These students will also find examples from text and generate questions. After students have prepared for the trial, you will sit in the middle of the two sides. Each side will choose a spokesperson to ask questions and try to prove their point about your ability to present the information in a balanced manner.

Mr. Leppo's 11th-grade science class has a current events segment for students to examine up-to-date science issues. Some recent science articles are analyzing the find of fossils in Utah and what they mean for the current views on the age of the land bridge. The following is Candace's worksheet:

### Interview Worksheet

**Topic:** *Fossil finds in Utah*

| **Facts from the text** | **Questions for the author** |
|---|---|
| *Scientists recently found two new versions of a species of dinosaurs called ankylosaur.* | *Why is this find important?* |
| *The bones were several million years older than any other version of the same species. The volcanic ash helps determine the age of the dinosaurs.* | *How certain are the scientists about dating the age of dinosaurs through examining volcanic ash?* |
| *Because of the age of the dinosaurs, it was determined that the land bridge was much older than originally believed.* | *How will this information impact other beliefs about dinosaurs and our prehistory?* |

### Activity 8: Looking at Text Features

Choose text that has many text features. Magazines and newspapers designed for kids work well for this activity. Introduce the students to a list of text features. Give them some magazines to look at and ask if they see any features that need to be added to the list. Finally, have them answer the following questions about the effect(s) that text features have on the audience:

1. Choose your favorite text feature. Why is this your favorite feature?

2. Why did the author choose this feature?

3. Does this feature enhance your understanding of the information in the article? How? Remember to use specific text to support your reasons.

4. As a whole, do the text features enhance or detract from your understanding of the text? Explain.

5. What text feature would you add to further enhance your understanding of the text? Design the feature.

6. Would the author agree that the feature you want to add would enhance the text and clarify the reader's understanding of the issue or concept? Why or why not?

## Activity 9: Audience Portraits

Although it is important for the reader to be able to visualize the author and understand his or her purpose and choices, it is also important that students realize that effective authors will visualize and analyze the audience to appeal to its needs, beliefs, and interests. Have the students create a portrait of a probable audience member by drawing the head and shoulders. Have the students add thought bubbles around the audience member's head, and have the students write information related to the audience's values and beliefs by using the following questions as a springboard for brainstorming:

- What does the audience believe about the topic?
- What is important to the audience?
- What questions will the audience have about the topic?
- How will the audience respond to the author's message?

## Activity 10: Author's Résumé

Have students research the life of the author. Then, have the students assume the persona of the author and write a résumé about the author's life. The categories for the résumé may include

- Education
- Jobs and career choices
- Accomplishments

Discuss with the students how the author's life affects his or her ideas and viewpoints that they are encountering in the text. If you do not have any information about the author, have the students create a "mock" résumé and make logical inferences about the author's life based on the way he or she presents information, his or her knowledge base, and his or her apparent viewpoint on the topic.

## Activity 11: Double-Entry Journal
## for Evaluating the Author's Viewpoint

Have the students begin by identifying the topic or concept they are studying. On the left side of the journal, have the students record the author's beliefs on the topic. On the right side of the journal, have the students reflect on their own beliefs about the topic and how the author's perspective influenced their own perspective.

Mr. Rinehart's ninth-grade history class is doing research on Native Americans and is examining the issues surrounding land confiscated by the government from the Native Americans. Jerome's worksheet is included here:

### *Evaluating the Author's Viewpoint: Double-Entry Journal*

**Topic:** *Native American land ownership*

| Text information | Reader's response |
|---|---|
| What does the author believe about the concept? Give specific text examples that reveal the author's beliefs. | What do I believe about the concept? |
| *The author believes that a sacred mountain belongs to 481 members of a Native American community living in Albuquerque.* | *I agree with the author. I believe that a lot of land has been taken from the Native Americans over the years so they should have it back.* |
| *Several visitors are concerned because they believe that they will not be allowed to freely visit the site anymore.* | *But I also think that two groups of people can share the land and be nice to each other.* |
| *The author believes that visitors and Native Americans can peaceably share the land.* | |

How are the author's beliefs and my beliefs about the topic similar? Different? Did my beliefs change after reading? How?

*My beliefs are very similar to the author's beliefs. I did not have much of an opinion before I did some research. But now I agree with the author. The next time I read about this topic, I will have an opinion about it.*

## ASSESSING STUDENT MASTERY OF EVALUATING THE AUTHOR'S VIEWPOINT

As teachers, we understand the importance of assessing whether or not students have acquired the skill that has been taught. You may choose to use one, many, or all of the activities presented in this chapter to help students become more proficient with evaluating the author's viewpoint. As a professional, you will make observations regarding students' acquisition of this skill, but it is also important to formally assess their knowledge and understanding.

Here, you will find a generic rubric for assessing the skill of evaluating authors' beliefs, opinions, or points of view in their writing.

## Understanding the Author's Viewpoint Rubric

Use this rubric as an assessment tool to determine your students' progress toward mastering the following objective: The student understands the author's viewpoint in various forms of text.

### Level 4—Mastery

- The student thoroughly and accurately differentiates between fact and the author's opinion.
- The student understands the author's purpose for writing.
- The student thoroughly and accurately understands the author's word choice.
- The student uses context in which the text was written to determine the author's viewpoint.
- The student independently applies strategies for assessing the author's viewpoint.

### Level 3—Nearing Mastery

- The student differentiates between fact and the author's opinion with most pieces of text.
- The student understands the author's purpose for writing.
- The student understands the author's word choice in most texts.
- The student uses the context in which the text was written to determine the author's viewpoint with some guidance from the teacher.
- The student applies some strategies for assessing the author's viewpoint.

### Level 2—Developing

- The student differentiates between fact and the author's opinion with much guidance from a teacher.
- The student understands the author's purpose for writing with guidance from a teacher.
- The student attempts to understand the author's word choice with guidance from a teacher.

### Level 1—Basic

- The student has difficulty differentiating between fact and the author's opinion.
- The student struggles to understand the author's purpose for writing.
- The student struggles to understand the author's word choice.

### Level 0—Below Basic

- The student makes no attempt to understand the author's viewpoint.

# Resource:

## Reproducible Worksheets
## for Chapter Activities

# CHAPTER 2: SETTING A PURPOSE FOR READING

## Yes/No Evaluation

**Purpose for Reading:** _____

| Questions About the Topic | Answers (Based on Reading and Research) |
|---|---|
|  |  |

## Yes/No Evaluation

| Did you achieve your purpose for reading?  Explain. |
|---|
|  |

# Question, Answer, Opinion

| Question: |
| --- |
| Answer: |
| Opinion: |

| Question: |
| --- |
| Answer: |
| Opinion: |

## Purpose for Reading Double-Entry Journal

**Purpose for Reading Question:** _____

> **Key:**
>
> P! = Strong Connection to Purpose for Reading
>
> P = Some Connection to Purpose for Reading

| Text Information With Code | How does this information connect with your purpose for reading or your prior knowledge of the subject? What questions do you have? |
|---|---|
| | |
| | |
| | |

# Multiple Text Marathon

| Purpose for Reading: | Best text?<br>Place a ✓ |
|---|---|
| **Evaluation of Text 1:**<br><br>This article will/will not achieve my purpose because . . . | |
| **Evaluation of Text 2:**<br><br>This article will/will not achieve my purpose because . . . | |
| **Evaluation of Text 3:**<br><br>This article will/will not achieve my purpose because . . . | |

# Author and Me Analysis

**My Purpose for Reading:** _____

| Information From the Text | Author's Purpose |
|---|---|
|  |  |

# Fact-Finding Mission

**Purpose for Reading:** _____

| Ideas and Facts | My Reaction |
|---|---|
| | |

# Persuasion Puzzles

| Persuasive Text Information | Author's Persuasive Techniques |
|---|---|
|  |  |

| Reaction to the Author's Techniques | Questions for Further Study |
|---|---|
|  |  |

# KWL Purpose Chart

| Before Reading: What do you already know about the topic? | Before Reading: What do you want to know about the topic? | After Reading: What did you learn? |
| --- | --- | --- |
| | | |

## Analysis of Directions

**Purpose for Directions:** _____

| Set of Directions | Analysis of Directions (Questions, areas of confusion, things I needed to know) |
|---|---|
| | |

# CHAPTER 3: CONNECTING TO PRIOR KNOWLEDGE

## Double-Entry Journal for Prior Knowledge

**Topic:** _____

**Prior Knowledge of the Topic:** _____

| Text Information | Reader's Response |
|---|---|
| What are the three most important things you have learned from the text? | What further questions do you have? |

# Structured Preview

**Topic:** _____

| Text Information | Questions, Thoughts, Reactions |
|---|---|
| **Text Structure:** | |
| **Text Features:** | |
| **Bolded Vocabulary or Information:** | |

# Predicting and Confirming

**Topic:** _____

| Before Reading Prediction Statement | During Reading Yes/No | After Reading Reaction Statement |
|---|---|---|
| | | I was surprised when . . . <br><br> I was confused when . . . <br><br> I was disappointed when . . . |

**Topic:** _____

| Before Reading Prediction Statement | During Reading Yes/No | After Reading Reaction Statement |
|---|---|---|
| | | I was surprised when . . . <br><br> I was confused when . . . <br><br> I was disappointed when . . . |

## A Reading Action Plan

**Topic:** _____

| Words you know that are connected to the topic | What do you think you know about these words? |
|---|---|
|  |  |
|  |  |
|  |  |
|  |  |

**Write a summary of what you think you know about the topic:**

**What do you expect to learn?**

**What did you learn?**

# Viewpoint Synthesizer

**Topic:** _____

| | |
|---|---|
| **The Author's Viewpoint (Summary):** | **The Teacher's Viewpoint (Summary):** |
| **Another Source's Viewpoint (Summary):** | **A Classmate's Viewpoint (Summary):** |

**My Viewpoint on the Topic:**

## KWL Chart PLUS Reflection

**Topic:** _____

| Before Reading: What do you already know about the topic? | Before Reading: What do you want to know about the topic? | After Reading: What did you learn? |
|---|---|---|
| | | |

**Plus:** What further questions do you have? How can you use the information you have learned? What surprised you about the information?

## Historical Fiction Anticipation Guide

**Directions:** Before you begin reading the story or novel, complete the "Before Reading" portion of this anticipation guide. After you have finished reading, complete the "After Reading" portion of this anticipation guide.

| Before Reading | Theme | After Reading |
|---|---|---|
| Agree  Disagree | Historical figures experience the same feelings that I do. | Agree  Disagree |
| Agree  Disagree | Historical figures experience different feelings than I do. | Agree  Disagree |
| Agree  Disagree | Events in history make the people who experience those events feel many things. | Agree  Disagree |
| Agree  Disagree | Authors write historical fiction to help us learn about how people felt about the things that were happening to them. | Agree  Disagree |
| Agree  Disagree | I can relate to other people regardless of the time period in which they lived. | Agree  Disagree |
| Agree  Disagree | I can relate to other people regardless of their race or ethnicity. | Agree  Disagree |
| Agree  Disagree | I can relate to other people regardless of their gender. | Agree  Disagree |
| Agree  Disagree | I can relate to other people regardless of their beliefs. | Agree  Disagree |
| Agree  Disagree | Historical fiction helps us to develop empathy with people who lived in different time periods. | Agree  Disagree |

**Reflection:** What is the most important theme you have learned? How does this theme help you to better understand the genre of historical fiction?

# CHAPTER 4: UNDERSTANDING VOCABULARY TERMS AND CONCEPTS

## Double-Entry Journal for Defining Vocabulary

**Purpose:** _____

| Text Information | Reader's Response |
|---|---|
| List words that are unfamiliar to you. | Use a dictionary to define each of the words. |

# Attribute Chart

**Topic or Concept:** _____

| In the columns to the right, please write the titles of the books you read. ⇨  <br><br> On the lines below, write the list of attributes and continue to check and revise as you continue to read more books in the genre. ⇩ | | | | | | | |
|---|---|---|---|---|---|---|---|
| | | | | | | | |
| | | | | | | | |
| | | | | | | | |
| | | | | | | | |
| | | | | | | | |
| | | | | | | | |
| | | | | | | | |
| | | | | | | | |
| | | | | | | | |
| | | | | | | | |

## Question Cubes

| Identify the unknown word and its definition: | How does it connect to your personal experience? |
|---|---|
| Draw a picture of the word: | Where might you encounter this word again? |

| Identify the unknown word and its definition: | How does it connect to your personal experience? |
|---|---|
| Draw a picture of the word: | Where might you encounter this word again? |

## Cartoon Worksheet

| Scene 1: | Scene 2: | Scene 3: |
|---|---|---|
| | | |
| Scene 4: | Scene 5: | Scene 6: |
| | | |

## Concept

**Map**

# Vocabulary Capsule

**Topic:** _____

**Before Reading Capsule of Key Vocabulary:** _____



**Before Reading Story or Paragraph Using the Capsule Words:**



**After Reading Story or Paragraph Using the Capsule Words:**

# CHAPTER 5: IDENTIFYING SIGNIFICANT INFORMATION IN TEXT

## Using Notecards

| |
|---|
| **Key Concept:**<br><br><br>**Main Idea:**<br><br><br>**Supporting Details:**<br><br><br>**Source:**<br><br><br>**Evaluation of Information:**<br><br> |

| |
|---|
| **Key Concept:**<br><br><br>**Main Idea:**<br><br><br>**Supporting Details:**<br><br><br>**Source:**<br><br><br>**Evaluation of Information:**<br><br> |

## Put a Box Around What's Important

**Topic:** _____

| Bracketed Information and Key Word | Personal Response |
|---|---|
| | This information is important because . . .<br>I can remember this information by . . .<br>I wonder . . . |
| | |

# Trifold Note Taking

**Topic:** _____

---

**Before Reading**

Describe the headings, subheadings, bolded words, charts, captions, and diagrams.

What do you predict you will be learning?

---

**During Reading**

What are you learning? What surprises, interests, or confuses you?

---

**After Reading**

Demonstrate your learning by drawing a picture, writing a summary, or writing a diary entry.

---

# Key Word Note Taking

**Topic:** _____

| Key Word | Definition | Examples |
|---|---|---|
|  |  |  |
|  |  |  |
|  |  |  |
|  |  |  |
|  |  |  |
|  |  |  |
|  |  |  |
|  |  |  |
|  |  |  |

## Cornell Notes

**Topic:** _____

| Key Words | Definitions and Explanations |
|-----------|------------------------------|
|           |                              |
|           |                              |
|           |                              |

## Double-Entry Journal for Identifying Significant Information

What is the key concept you are investigating?

| Text Information | Reader's Response |
|---|---|
| What important information connects to the key concept? Use headings, subheadings, and bolded words to help you. | Draw a picture or a symbol that represents your understanding of the important information in the text. |

# CHAPTER 6: VISUALIZING TEXT INFORMATION

## Analyzing Imagery

| Text Information | Reader's Response |
|---|---|
| **Directions:** On the left side of the double-entry journal, you will record examples of imagery. You can do this in a number of ways including: | **Directions:** On the right side of the double-entry journal, you will be responding to what you have read. You can do this in many ways including: |
| **Making a list:** You can make a list of words and phrases that evoke images in your mind. Remember these words and phrases will appeal to your five senses. The author will also use figurative language to create images in your mind about the setting and characters. | **Identifying the senses to which the author is appealing:** Descriptions and figurative language appeal to one or more of a reader's five senses: sight, sound, taste, touch, smell. |
| **Copying a passage:** You can copy an entire passage that appeals to the five senses. This passage will have adjectives, vivid verbs, and possibly figurative language. Authors usually use imagery when describing settings, characters, and action scenes. Remember to use quotation marks when copying someone else's words. | **Writing a personal response:** When you respond personally, you write about a similar experience or memory that you have had that relates to the information in the text.<br><br>**Writing an analytical response:** When you respond analytically, you critique the author's style, word choice, sequencing of events, character development, and use of text structure and text features. |
| **Recording:** Record the page number, paragraph number, and or chapter from which you took the information. | **Asking questions:** You can question the author, the teacher, or yourself. Generally, you will question things that you do not understand or things that confuse you in order to gain a greater understanding of new concepts. |

# Imagery Double-Entry Journal Sentence Starters

**Directions:** As you complete your responses on the right side of the double-entry journal, you may use the following sentence starters to help you write excellent responses. You do not have to use the sentence starters!

## Personal Response Sentence Starters:

This passage reminds me of the time when . . .

This passage reminds me of a place where . . .

This passage makes me feel _____ because . . .

These words/phrases make me think of . . .

## Analytical Response Sentence Starters:

I think this passage shows imagery because . . .

This passage is significant because . . .

The description in this passage makes me think that _____
will happen next because . . .

The author is using this imagery to establish a _____ mood because . . .

The author is using sensory detail because . . .

The author is using this simile/metaphor to make the reader think of . . .

The author is using this simile/metaphor to compare . . .

The author is using personification because . . .

The author is using the color _____ because . . .

I think the author does a (good, poor) job using imagery because . . .

I think this passage could be improved by using imagery in the following way . . .

## Visualizing Text Information—Double-Entry Journal Adaptation

**Directions:** As you read, record a passage that includes a lot of sensory detail and then either draw or describe the image that's in your head.

| Quote or list of sensory details from the text | Drawing that shows what's in your head or description that includes details that are not in the text |
|---|---|
| | |

My Response: This image reminds me of . . .

# Double-Entry Journal for Analyzing Characters

Title of book, poem, story, or article: _____

Author's name: _____

Theme focus: _____

| Text Information | Reader's Response |
|---|---|
| **Directions:** On the left side of the double-entry journal, you will record examples of characterization. You can do this in a number of ways including: <br><br> **Making a list:** You can make a list of words and phrases that reveal character traits. Authors reveal character traits through: <br><br> ❏ description, <br> ❏ the character's actions, <br> ❏ thoughts and feelings, <br> ❏ dialogue, <br> ❏ the actions and feelings of other characters. <br><br> **Copying a passage:** You can copy an entire passage that reveals character traits. You may copy a passage that reveals the character's actions, thoughts, or feelings. You may record a passage of dialogue that reveals the character's traits. Remember to use quotation marks when copying someone else's words. <br><br> **Recording:** Record the page number, paragraph number, and/or chapter from which you took the information. | **Directions:** On the right side of the double-entry journal, you will be responding to what you have read. You can do this in a number of ways including: <br><br> **Identifying the character traits that are revealed:** One of the things that authors do is "show don't tell." If a character throws a chair across the room, the reader can infer that the character is angry even if the author never actually used the word "angry" to describe the character. <br><br> **Writing a personal response:** When you respond personally, you write about a similar experience or memory that you have had that relates to the information in the text. Most likely, you will not be able to connect with specific events in the book, but you will be able to connect with the emotions of the main character. You may relate a similar experience in this section or agree/disagree with the character's behavior. <br><br> **Writing an analytical response:** When you respond analytically, you critique the author's style, word choice, sequencing of events, character development, and use of text structure and text features. <br><br> **Asking questions:** You can question the author, the teacher, or yourself. Generally, you will question things that you do not understand, things that confuse you, or things that you have never thought about in order to gain a greater understanding of new concepts. |

_____'s Bookmark

As you read this book, you will be recording examples of imagery on this bookmark. On the line under pg. and par., record a brief notation to yourself about the passage. You will be responding in detail to these passages in your double-entry journal.

pg. _____ par. _____
pg. _____ par. _____
pg. _____ par. _____
pg. _____ par. _____
pg. _____ par. _____
pg. _____ par. _____
pg. _____ par. _____
pg. _____ par. _____
pg. _____ par. _____

_____'s Bookmark

As you read this book, you will be recording examples of imagery on this bookmark. On the line under pg. and par., record a brief notation to yourself about the passage. You will be responding in detail to these passages in your double-entry journal.

pg. _____ par. _____
pg. _____ par. _____
pg. _____ par. _____
pg. _____ par. _____
pg. _____ par. _____
pg. _____ par. _____
pg. _____ par. _____
pg. _____ par. _____

_____'s Bookmark

As you read this book, you will be recording examples of imagery on this bookmark. On the line under pg. and par., record a brief notation to yourself about the passage. You will be responding in detail to these passages in your double-entry journal.

pg. _____ par. _____
pg. _____ par. _____
pg. _____ par. _____
pg. _____ par. _____
pg. _____ par. _____
pg. _____ par. _____
pg. _____ par. _____
pg. _____ par. _____

_____'s Bookmark

As you read this book, you will be recording examples of imagery on this bookmark. On the line under pg. and par., record a brief notation to yourself about the passage. You will be responding in detail to these passages in your double-entry journal.

pg. _____ par. _____
pg. _____ par. _____
pg. _____ par. _____
pg. _____ par. _____
pg. _____ par. _____
pg. _____ par. _____
pg. _____ par. _____
pg. _____ par. _____

**145**

## Imagery and Figurative Language Focus

Imagery is defined as "artistic" words, phrases, and passages that create a mental picture in the reader's mind. Literary devices that authors use to create pictures in the reader's mind include:

Adjectives
Vivid action verbs
Figurative language

Figurative language tools include:

Similes
Metaphors
Personification
Onomatopoeia
Hyperbole

Adjectives and sensory details might include:

Colors (be aware of negative and positive connotations)
Dark vs. Light
Shapes and Sizes
Textures/Temperatures
Aromas

You will find imagery in descriptions of:

Setting, Character, Action, Animals, Objects

## Imagery and Figurative Language Focus

Imagery is defined as "artistic" words, phrases, and passages that create a mental picture in the reader's mind. Literary devices that authors use to create pictures in the reader's mind include:

Adjectives
Vivid action verbs
Figurative language

Figurative language tools include:

Similes
Metaphors
Personification
Onomatopoeia
Hyperbole

Adjectives and sensory details might include:

Colors (be aware of negative and positive connotations)
Dark vs. Light
Shapes and Sizes
Textures/Temperatures
Aromas

You will find imagery in descriptions of:

Setting, Character, Action, Animals, Objects

## Imagery and Figurative Language Focus

Imagery is defined as "artistic" words, phrases, and passages that create a mental picture in the reader's mind. Literary devices that authors use to create pictures in the reader's mind include:

Adjectives
Vivid action verbs
Figurative language

Figurative language tools include:

Similes
Metaphors
Personification
Onomatopoeia
Hyperbole

Adjectives and sensory details might include:

Colors (be aware of negative and positive connotations)
Dark vs. Light
Shapes and Sizes
Textures/Temperatures
Aromas

You will find imagery in descriptions of:

Setting, Character, Action, Animals, Objects

## Imagery and Figurative Language Focus

Imagery is defined as "artistic" words, phrases, and passages that create a mental picture in the reader's mind. Literary devices that authors use to create pictures in the reader's mind include:

Adjectives
Vivid action verbs
Figurative language

Figurative language tools include:

Similes
Metaphors
Personification
Onomatopoeia
Hyperbole

Adjectives and sensory details might include:

Colors (be aware of negative and positive connotations)
Dark vs. Light
Shapes and Sizes
Textures/Temperatures
Aromas

You will find imagery in descriptions of:

Setting, Character, Action, Animals, Objects

# Character Double-Entry Journal Sentence Starters

**Directions:** As you complete your responses on the right side of the double-entry journal, you may use the following sentence starters to help you write excellent responses. Use the sentence starters for guidance.

**Personal Response Sentence Starters:**

This character reminds me of myself when . . .

This character reminds me of . . . (relatives, friends, teachers, acquaintances, character in book, movie, and TV)

This character's actions remind me of a time when . . .

This character believes what I believed when . . .

I had a similar conflict/situation when . . .

I would have handled the situation the same/differently because . . .

I agree/disagree with the character's decision to . . .

**Analytical Response Sentence Starters:**

The most important character in the story is _____ because . . .

My character feels _____ when _____ happens because . . .

A problem that my character has is _____. I know this problem is significant because . . .

A message that the author is trying to give through the character's actions is . . .
I know this because . . .

My character's attitude about _____ is _____.
I know this because . . .

I think my character will . . .

My character said _____ because . . .

To solve his/her problem, the character should . . . (list the steps the character should take to solve the problem)

I think the character's behavior is changing because . . .

# Characterization – Student Resource Page

*Characterization* – Characters are defined by their physical traits and character traits. Physical traits describe the way that a character looks (the outer-self) and character traits describe the way a character feels and behaves (the inner-self). An author creates a character by using one or more of the following elements of characterization:

- ❑ Descriptive details
- ❑ Actions/behavior of the character
- ❑ Thoughts and feelings of the character

- ❑ Dialogue
- ❑ Actions/thoughts/feelings of other characters

## *Words That Describe How Characters Behave:*

Directions: Read each adjective that describes how characters act and determine if the adjective is generally positive or negative by putting a plus (+) or minus (−) sign next to each adjective.

| | | | |
|---|---|---|---|
| Agreeable | Enthusiastic | Kind | Self-centered |
| Aggressive | Fearless | Lazy | Selfish |
| Ambitious | Flexible | Loyal | Sensible |
| Angry | Foolish | Merciful | Serious |
| Appreciative | Friendly | Mischievous | Servile |
| Argumentative | Generous | Modest | Shy |
| Arrogant | Gentle | Narrow-minded | Sincere |
| Bashful | Greedy | Noble | Stubborn |
| Boastful | Grouchy | Obedient | Subservient |
| Brave | Gullible | Observant | Superstitious |
| Calculating | Hardworking | Overconfident | Suspicious |
| Candid | Honest | Patient | Thoughtful |
| Cautious | Honorable | Perceptive | Thoughtless |
| Clever | Humble | Persistent | Timid |
| Conceited | Humorous | Proud | Trusting |
| Confident | Imaginative | Reasonable | Uncooperative |
| Considerate | Impatient | Reliable | Understanding |
| Cooperative | Impulsive | Responsible | Unreasonable |
| Courageous | Inconsiderate | Rigid | Unselfish |
| Curious | Independent | Sarcastic | Wise |
| Deceitful | Industrious | Scornful | |
| Determined | Insecure | Self-conscious | |
| Dishonest | Insincere | Self-sacrificing | |

RESOURCE **149**

# CHAPTER 7: ASKING QUESTIONS IN ORDER
# TO DEVELOP A DEEPER UNDERSTANDING

## Trivial Pursuit

**Topic:** _____

| Concept | Question | Answer | Inference Required? (Yes/No) |
|---|---|---|---|
|  |  |  |  |
|  |  |  |  |
|  |  |  |  |
|  |  |  |  |
|  |  |  |  |
|  |  |  |  |
|  |  |  |  |

# Partners-Question

**Topic:** _____

| Questions | Answers |
|---|---|
| **Partner #1 Question:** | |
| **Partner #2 Question:** | |
| **Partner #1 Question:** | |
| **Partner #2 Question:** | |
| **Partner #1 Question:** | |
| **Partner #2 Question:** | |

## An Archaeological Dig

**Topic:** _____

| Before Reading Questions | |
| --- | --- |
| **During Reading Questions** | **Responses** |
| | |

| After Reading Synthesis |
| --- |
| |

# QAR Bookmarks

| Front of Bookmark | Back of Bookmark |
|---|---|
| As you read this text, you will be recording examples of important information needed to answer your questions. On the line under pg. and par., record a brief notation to yourself about the passage. Remember to think about the question/answer relationship.<br><br>pg._____ par._____<br><br>_____<br><br>pg._____ par._____<br><br>_____<br><br>pg._____ par._____<br><br>_____<br><br>pg._____ par._____<br><br>_____<br><br>pg._____ par._____<br><br>_____<br><br>pg._____ par._____<br><br>_____<br><br>pg._____ par._____<br><br>_____ | Purpose for Reading:<br>_____<br><br>**Key Words in Reading Questions:**<br><br>1. _____<br><br>2. _____<br><br>3. _____<br><br><br>1. **Right There:** Details are literal and easy for the reader to find.<br><br>2. **Think and Search:** Details are located throughout the text and the reader must be able to search the text for the answer(s) to the question.<br><br>3. **On My Own:** The reader must access prior knowledge about the topic and reading, make inferences, make connections between the text and prior knowledge, make connections between the text and other texts.<br><br>4. **Author and Me:** The reader must access prior knowledge about being an author in order to understand the choices and decisions of the author. |

# CHAPTER 8: DRAWING CONCLUSIONS AND MAKING INFERENCES

## Text as Words or Images

**Topic:** _____

| Text as Words (In Your Own Words) | Text as Images (From Your Own Mind) |
| --- | --- |
|  |  |

# Inferencing Cubes

**Topic:** _____

| People | Events |
|---|---|
|  |  |
| **Settings (Time and Place)** | **Other Important Facts** |
|  |  |

**Inference (Why is this information important?):**

## Double-Entry Journal for Drawing Conclusions

**Purpose for Reading:** _____

| Text Information | Reader's Response |
|---|---|
| What information from the text matches your purpose for reading? | What conclusion can you draw about the concept you are studying? What conclusion can you draw about the author? |

# CHAPTER 9: ANALYZING TEXT STRUCTURE

## Text Structure Chart

| Text Structure | Definition | Key Structure Words |
|---|---|---|
| Description | Author gives examples and details to better describe a topic. | For example, for instance, specifically, in addition |
| Sequence/Narrative | Author writes the main idea and details in a specific order. Examples: chronological; order of importance | First, second, third, then, next, another, additionally, at last, in conclusion, before, after, later, in the beginning, in the end |
| Cause/Effect | Author presents a topic or issue and shows the relationship between the causes and effects related to the topic or issue. | If, then; consequently; because, then; as a result; therefore |
| Comparison/Contrast | Author presents a topic or issue and shows the similarities and differences between subtopics related to the topic. | Similarly, on the other hand, but, by contrast, in the same manner, as opposed to |
| Problem/Solution | Author presents a problem and provides a solution often through argument. | However, therefore, in addition |

# Sequence Planner for Skit

**Student Partners:** _____

**Purpose:** _____

| Characters: |
| --- |
| |

| Setting: |
| --- |
| |

**Sequence Planner:**

| Event #1: |
| --- |
| **Event #2:** |
| **Event #3:** |
| **Event #4:** |
| **Event #5:** |

**Prediction about next event:**

**Performance notes:**

# Dramatic Predictions

**Event:** _____

| Summary of Dramatic Prediction (What will happen next?) | Confirmation or Contradiction Based on Text |
|---|---|
|  |  |

**Event:** _____

| Summary of Dramatic Prediction (What will happen next?) | Confirmation or Contradiction Based on Text |
|---|---|
|  |  |

**Event:** _____

| Summary of Dramatic Prediction (What will happen next?) | Confirmation or Contradiction Based on Text |
|---|---|
|  |  |

# Cause-Effect Relationships

**Topic:** _____

| Cause | Effect |
|---|---|
|  |  |
|  |  |

**Topic:** _____

| Cause | Effect |
|---|---|
|  |  |
|  |  |

**Topic:** _____

| Cause | Effect |
|---|---|
|  |  |
|  |  |

# Analyzing Text Structure – Double-Entry Journal

**Passage One**

**Topic:** _____

**Purpose for Reading:** _____

| Text Information | Reader's Response |
|---|---|
| What key words and organizational techniques can help you identify the text structure? | Did the author select the best structure for sharing the information? Explain. Did the text structure help you to achieve your purpose for reading? Explain. |

**Passage Two**

**Topic:** _____

**Purpose for Reading:** _____

| Text Information | Reader's Response |
|---|---|
| What key words and organizational techniques can help you identify the text structure? | Did the author select the best structure for sharing the information? Explain. Did the text structure help you to achieve your purpose for reading? Explain. |

## CHAPTER 10: EVALUATING THE AUTHOR'S VIEWPOINT

### My Opinion/the Author's Opinion

Topic: _____

Purpose: _____

| Facts From the Text | The Author's Opinion of the Topic | The Reader's Opinion of the Topic |
|---|---|---|
|  |  |  |
|  |  |  |
|  |  |  |

## Interview Worksheet

**Topic:** _____

| Facts From the Text | Questions for the Author |
|---|---|
| | |
| | |
| | |
| | |
| | |

## Evaluating Author's Viewpoint – Double-Entry Journal

**Topic:** _____

| Text Information | Reader's Response |
|---|---|
| What does the author believe about the concept? Give specific text examples that reveal the author's beliefs. | What do I believe about the concept? |

How are the author's beliefs and my beliefs about the topic similar? Different? Did my beliefs change after reading? How?

# References and Suggested Reading

Bradbury, R. (1991). All summer in a day. In *Prentice Hall Literature, Bronze Edition.* Englewood Cliffs, NJ: Prentice Hall.

Calkins, L. (1997). *Raising lifelong learners.* Reading, MA: Addison-Wesley.

Calkins, L. M., & Harwayne, S. (1990). *Living between the lines.* Portsmouth, NH: Heinemann.

Crist, B. I. (1975). One capsule a week: A painless remedy for vocabulary ills. *Journal of Reading, 19,* 147–149.

Davey, B. (1983). Think-aloud: Modeling the cognitive processes of reading comprehension. *Journal of Reading, 27,* 44–47.

Enciso, P. (1990). *The nature of engagement in reading: Profiles of three fifth graders' engagement strategies and stances.* Unpublished doctoral dissertation, Ohio State University, Columbus.

Gillet, J. W., & Temple, C. (1990). *Understanding reading problems: Assessment and instruction* (3rd ed.). Glenview, IL/Boston: Scott, Foresman/Little, Brown.

Harvey, S., & Goudvis, A. (2000). *Strategies that work: Teaching comprehension to enhance understanding.* York, ME: Stenhouse.

Hurd, D., et al. (1991). Kinetic and potential energy. In *Physical science* (pp. 375–382). Englewood Cliffs, NJ: Prentice Hall.

Ignoffo, M. (1993/1994). Theatre of the mind: Nonconventional strategies for helping remedial readers gain control over their reading experience. *Journal of Reading, 37,* 4.

International Reading Association/National Council of Teachers of English. (1996). *Standards for the English language arts.* Newark, DE/Urbana, IL: Author.

Irvin, J. (1990). *Reading and the middle school student: Strategies to enhance literacy.* Boston: Allyn & Bacon.

Irvin, J. (1998). *Reading and the middle school student: Strategies to enhance literacy* (2nd ed.). Boston: Allyn & Bacon.

James, S. (1990a). Battles and defense. In *Eyewitness books: Ancient Rome* (pp. 12–13). New York: Knopf.

James, S. (1990b). Writing it all down. In *Eyewitness books: Ancient Rome* (pp. 40–41). New York: Knopf.

Johnson, D. D., & Pearson, P. D. (1978). *Teaching reading vocabulary.* New York: Holt, Rinehart & Winston.

Lane, B. (1993). *After the end.* Portsmouth, NH: Heinemann.

Langer, J. A. (1995). *Envisioning literature: Literary understanding and literature instruction.* New York: Teachers College Press.

Langer, J. A. (1998, February). Thinking and doing literature: An eight year study. *English Journal,* 16–23.

Langer, J. A., & Applebee, A. N. (1987). *How writing shapes thinking.* Urbana, IL: National Council of Teachers of English.

Marr, M. B., & Gormley, K. (1982). Children's recall of familiar and unfamiliar text. *Reading Research Quarterly, 18,* 80–104.

Ogle, D. M. (1986). K-W-L: A teaching model that develops active reading of expository text. *The Reading Teacher, 39*(6), 564–570.

Parker, S. (1990). Plants at the pond's surface. In *Eyewitness Books: Pond & River* (pp. 44–45). New York: Knopf.

Paterson, K. (1978). *The great Gilly Hopkins.* New York: HarperCollins.

Pauk, W., & Owens, R. J. Q. (2004). *How to study in college* (8th ed.). Boston: Houghton Mifflin.

Paulsen, G. (1987). *Hatchet.* New York: Puffin.

Pearson, P. D. (1985). *The comprehension revolution: A twenty-five year history of process and practice related to reading comprehension* (Reading Education Report No. 57). Champaign: University of Illinois, Center for the Study of Reading.

Pressley, M., Brown, R., Beard El-Dinary, P., & Afflerbach, P. (1995). The comprehension instruction that students need: Instruction fostering constructively responsive reading. *Learning Disabilities Research & Practice, 10*(4), 215–224.

Pressley, M., Brown, R., Van Meter, P., & Schuder, T. (1995). Trends: Reading/transactional strategies. *Educational Leadership, 52*(8), 81.

Spiro, R. J. (1968). Constructive processes in prose comprehension and recall. In R. J. Spiro, B. C. Bruce, & W. F. Brewer (Eds.), *Theoretical issues in reading comprehension.* Hillsdale, NJ: Lawrence Erlbaum.

Teacher Created Materials/Time, Inc. (2000). *Should students wear school uniforms?* Westminster, CA/New York: Author.

Thomas, S. K., & Wilson, M. (1993). Idiosyncratic interpretations: Negotiating meaning in expository prose. *English Journal, 82*(1), 58–64.

Vaughn, J. L., & Estes, T. H. (1986). *Reading and reasoning beyond the primary grades.* Boston: Allyn & Bacon.

Wilhelm, J. D. (1997). *You gotta be the book.* New York: Teacher's College, Columbia University.

Wittrock, M. C., Marks, C., & Doctorow, M. (1975). Reading as a generative process. *Journal of Educational Psychology, 67,* 484–489.

Youngblood, E. (1985, September). Reading, thinking, and writing using the reading journal. *English Journal, 74,* 46–48.

# Index